D0600758

To Margaret —
blessings in the open heart —
Richard Wehrman

HEARTWORK

HOW TO GET WHAT YOU REALLY, REALLY WANT

PRAISE FOR *HEARTWORK*

"There are in this world illnesses that seek healings in just the same way as aspirants seek liberation—the right catalyst is crucial. Dale Goldstein is just such a catalyst for healing."

> —Stephen Levine, author of *A Gradual Awakening* (Anchor Press, 1979), *Meetings at the Edge* (Anchor Press, 1984), and *Healing Into Life and Death* (Anchor Press, 1987)

"*Heartwork* gave me chills when I first picked up the manuscript. This wonderful book is simply the truth about what it takes to heal and become vibrantly healthy."

> —Christiane Northrup, M.D., author of *Mother-Daughter Wisdom* (Bantam, 2005), *The Wisdom of Menopause* (Bantam, 2001), and *Women's Bodies, Women's Wisdom* (Bantam, 1998)

"With *Heartwork*, Dale Goldstein has created an important addition to the growing body of work integrating modern therapeutic approaches with awareness practices from spiritual traditions. But this book—in which Goldstein's compassion, experience and wisdom come shining through—is also visually striking and aesthetically rich. It shimmers with beauty and a sense of grace transmitted. The practices *Heartwork* offers are simple and powerful, and anyone willing to take this journey is sure to have some direct tastes of what all hearts truly seek."

> —Russ Hudson, author with Don Richard Riso of *The Wisdom of the Enneagram* (Bantam, 1999)

"This amazing and ground-breaking book by the master psychotherapist Dale Goldstein distills a lifetime of brilliant wisdom into a deeply moving and loving manual for profound spiritual transformation. Far and away the best book on personal transformation I have ever read. Read this book and you will never be the same."

> —Kenneth Porter, M.D., President, Association for Spirituality and Psychotherapy

"Dale has gifted us with a beautiful synthesis of his personal experience, essential principles in psychotherapy and a basic understanding of spiritual teachings. *Heartwork* is a powerful invitation to readers to make fundamental personal change, pointing the direction, mapping the territory and supporting the journey. The descriptions of both content and process are specific, detailed, comprehensive and thorough. Through the creative inclusion of sensitive poetry, vivid illustration and the richness and poignancy of others' experience, the book calls us to reach deeply beyond our intellectual structure. In helping us learn 'What We Really, Really Want,' Dale also gives a glimpse of 'Who We Really Are.'"

—Burt Giges, M.D., President-Elect, Association for Applied Sport Psychology

"*Heartwork* is a manual for going deep into yourself and emerging transformed, an invaluable guidebook for self-discovery."

—Donna Thomson, author of *The Vibrant Life: Simple Meditations to Use Your Energy Effectively* (Sentient Publications, 2006)

"Dale's work is innovative and groundbreaking. It combines meditation, therapy, bodywork, music, language and more in a way that creates something new and fresh and healing. *Heartwork* captures the spirit of the work and is the next-best thing to being with Dale in person."

—Michael Hull, author of *Sun Dancing: A Spiritual Journey On The Red Road* (Inner Traditions, 2000)

"*Heartwork* is the one book to take on your spiritual journey. The author knows how hard it is to be afraid of something and not be aware that you're afraid. The work is on target: how to get to what you don't know is bothering you—and heal it."

—James O'Hern, author of *Honoring the Stones* (Curbstone Press, 2004)

Heartwork

HOW TO GET WHAT YOU REALLY, REALLY WANT

BY DALE L. GOLDSTEIN, LCSW

Illustrations by RICHARD WEHRMAN

HEARTWORK INSTITUTE, INC.

HEARTWORK: HOW TO GET WHAT YOU REALLY, REALLY WANT

Copyright © 2007 by Dale L. Goldstein, LCSW, and Richard Wehrman

Photo-illuminations by Richard Wehrman

All Rights Reserved.

Printed in China

First Edition

9 8 7 6 5 4 3 2 1

Copyrights and acknowledgements for poems and quotations follow the book on pages 170–171 and are an extension of this copyright page.

The illustrations in this book incorporate and make use of the creativity of numerous photographers without whose works this greater work could not exist. Credits and copyrights for these artists follow on pages 172–175 and are an extension of this copyright page.

Book design by Richard Wehrman
www.merlinwood.net

Edited by Katy Koontz

Published by:

HEARTWORK INSTITUTE, INC.
Rochester, New York
www.awakentheheart.org

Publisher's Cataloging-in-Publication Data

Goldstein, Dale L.
   Heartwork : how to get what you really, really want / by Dale L.
Goldstein ; illustrated by Richard Wehrman. — 1st ed. — Rochester,
N.Y. : Heartwork Institute, 2007.
     p. ; cm.
   ISBN-13: 978-0-9789606-1-2
   ISBN-10: 0-9789606-1-0
   Includes bibliographical references.
1. Self-actualization (Psychology) 2. Self-realization. 3. Self-perception.
4. Whole and parts (Psychology) 5. Self-help
techniques. I. Wehrman, Richard. II. Title.
   BF637.S4 G65 2007
   155.2—dc22 0705
                                 2007923620

For my father, Allan Goldstein,
whose favorite quotation was Shakespeare's
"This above all: to thine own self be true,"
whose favorite historical figure was
Abraham Lincoln (on whose assassination
day he died in 1998), and who passed
on to me a soul hunger for Truth.

...Then the day came
when the risk to remain
tight in a bud
was more painful
than the risk it took
to blossom...

ANAIS NIN

ACKNOWLEDGMENTS

First and foremost, I thank my good friend Richard Wehrman for his magnificent artwork, design and poetic contributions to this book. It would not be anything without him. Next, I thank my life partner, Carolyn Cerame, for her exquisite sensitivity, incredible intuition, deep insight and unending support. Next, I thank my parents, Allan Goldstein and Estelle Goldstein; my children, Devan Goldstein and Jessica Kamens; my sisters, Wynne Bouley and Jan Goldstein; and my grandmother, Lizzie Radlow—all of whom, each in their own ways, taught me about unconditional love. I also express my deep gratitude to my ex-wife Ellen Goldstein for insisting that I grow, for helping to birth and develop Heartwork and for sticking with me through the hardest times of my life. I also thank my dear friends, too numerous to list, but especially Paul Kuhl and Richard Wehrman, who for 35 years have given and continue to give me the love, support, understanding and challenging I've needed to continue on my path.

I also thank all my clients and students who have given themselves to the difficult and challenging work of trying to understand who they really are, thereby forcing me to look more deeply into aspects of my own being that I may have been ignoring. It continues to be a great privilege and honor to witness with awe, and facilitate to the best of my ability, your unfolding into your true nature.

Next, I wish to acknowledge my principal teachers. Alia Johnson, my teacher in the Diamond Approach, serves as an ongoing inspiration. I am eternally grateful to her for her wisdom, depth, breadth and maturity of character and for her unswerving commitment to my awakening to my true nature. She has both challenged and affirmed my understanding and continues to drive me—she would probably say "invite" me—ever deeper. Toni Packer saved my spiritual life by giving me the space, encouragement and guidance to find my own way. Philip Kapleau, my Zen teacher, taught me about frustration, pain, patience and perseverance. Fred Thompson, my first teacher, taught me how to meditate and how not to live.

Many thanks also to my primary therapists (Connie Donaldson, who has been bringing her wisdom and compassion to the highs and lows of my life for decades, and Bekah Murdock, who taught me that it's OK to feel my feelings completely).

I am deeply indebted to the Heartwork book committee, especially Kenneth Rich and Elise Buskey (co-chairs), and the dozens of others who put time and energy into manifesting this book and without whose efforts and wise counsel the book would never have seen fruition. I am equally indebted to the many individuals who had enough faith in this book to help finance its creation and production.

And, of course, the book wouldn't have been a book without the workshop participants and clients who submitted their experiences to share with the readers. My gratitude goes to each one of you, whether your stories are included here or not. And equal gratitude goes to all those who read and gave feedback on the manuscript in its formative stages and to those who proofread it before publication.

I want to give special thanks to the people over the years who have gone way out of their way to help Heartwork flourish, including my "angel" administrator, Annette Barron; present and past Heartwork executive directors Karen Cooper, Trish Andraszek, Patricia Dorland and Hallie Sawyers; the Heartwork steering committee; Heartwork's principal Texas sponsors Donna Berber, Philip Berber, Cis Dickson and Maribeth Price; and our Texas angels and event coordinators Joann Gorka and Margie Mensik and primary helpers Brenda Bailey, Elise Buskey, Emily Carpenter, Andy Clawson, Marcie Gass, Brenda Gleason, Doug Gorka, Clayton Lee, Donna Sue Lee, Diana Livingston, Traci Noge, Ken Rich, Spencer Richardson, Donna Ries, Brian Stovall, Janice Wagley, Elaine Webster and Jeanne Yamonaco. I want to thank Brian Cooper for helping Heartwork realize its organizational potential; Philip Berber, Jonathan Bregman, Brian Cooper, Peter Davidson, Ross Garber, Devan Goldstein, Les Gourwitz, Bruce Peters and Jeremy Seligman for their sage business advice; Les Gourwitz for his generous donation of time and talents in marketing and advertising through his Houston advertising agency, Smith and Jones; and Dr. William Craig, internist extraordinaire, who has partnered with me in bringing total health care to his patients.

I am deeply indebted to Stephen Levine; Christiane Northrup, M.D.; Russ Hudson; Kenneth Porter, M.D.; Burt Giges, M.D.; Donna Thomson; Michael Hull and James O'Hern for their willingness to review and endorse the book.

Special thanks to my good friend Todd Carter for his inspired Unwinding compositions. Thanks also to Juliet Van Otteren for her beautiful portraiture.

Finally, I want to thank my superb editor, Katy Koontz, for her expertise as an editor, her love and guidance, her support and encouragement, and the work she has done and continues to do on herself that allowed her to understand what I was trying to say in this book.

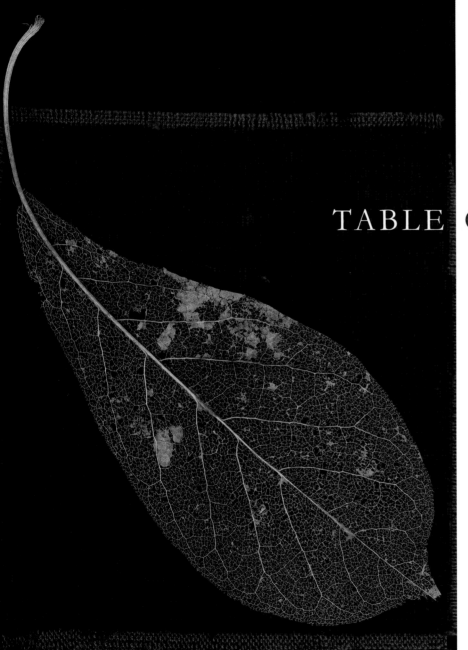

TABLE OF CONTENTS

PART I: INTRODUCTION

TO THE WORK

PRECAUTIONARY NOTE:

*This book is written in a specific and
deliberate order. For maximum benefit,
please do not skip any parts
and, especially,*

PLEASE DO NOT READ AHEAD.

I have lived on the lip

of insanity, wanting to know reasons,

knocking on a door. It opens.

I've been knocking from the inside!

—RUMI

The Descent

Life's spectator no longer could I be
And so myself did plunge
Through fear's dark sea:
Falling, drowning in despairing tears,
Ocean inhaling, sinking to unknown depths,
Imploding anguished cries I disappear into darkness
And am lost.

Then struggles cease,
Too tired to fight,
My being starts to yield,
Begins to pulse in rhythmic union
With all that once seemed foe,
Feeling with each heartbeat
Feared enemy becoming friend.

Then waves embrace and cradle,
Like loving arms enfolding,
As they lift their host up slowly,
In gentle reverent Hands,
Upward through shining rainbow hues,
Until, in one bright blinding flash,
I breathe the sun and hear earth sing
As I begin to dance.

—MARIBETH PRICE

This poem, written by a participant in the first Heartwork Intensive at the Omega Institute in July 1982, beautifully describes the experience of Heartwork. It shows the process Maribeth went through after a near-death experience due to an automobile accident. It also deftly conveys the spirit and transformational power of Heartwork as the primary contributor to her psychological and spiritual healing.

ABOUT HEARTWORK

Heartwork is a simple, direct, powerful yet gentle tool for opening fully to one's life. Both a counseling approach and a way of living, Heartwork serves to resolve problems at their core and to open the "heart of compassion."

Heartwork is a synthesis of Eastern meditative approaches to healing and Western psychotherapeutic techniques, using awareness as the primary vehicle to see into the source of one's problems.

The basic assumption of Heartwork is that our fundamental state is wholeness. Dis-ease is a separation from this wholeness.

What we identify as our problems are symptoms of underlying conflicts caused by running away from, or fighting against, certain aspects of ourselves. The tensions created by this internal split may manifest themselves as dis-ease in one or more of the interpenetrating aspects of our being: physical, emotional, mental and spiritual. In each case, these tensions are held in very specific places in the body/mind.

The solution to our perceived problems, then, is simply to stop running and to look directly into the heart of the problem by quieting the mind, clearly defining the problem, focusing the attention into the area of the body where the conflict seems to be located, and then looking into the very center of this area to find the resolution.

As you look more and more deeply into your experience of the problem, you become increasingly aware of the underlying mental, emotional and spiritual roots of the issue. By allowing yourself to be completely with these split-off parts, you will experience a coming together (a healing or "wholing") within yourself, in which the dis-ease–producing thought or feeling is released and the problem is resolved.

From this place of peace, you are then able to see clearly how you have moved away from your state of wholeness to create the problem that you have just resolved. Understanding, forgiveness and compassion flow freely from this insight, and healing (though not necessarily curing on a physical level) occurs naturally out of this inner ease. This awareness is then integrated into your actions, so that you can live more harmoniously with others and the world.

The Heartwork process teaches you to use life's problems as doorways into a space of open awareness and insight, rather than giving problems the power to run your life. As a result, you are continually learning from your experience, and life becomes "The Great Adventure."

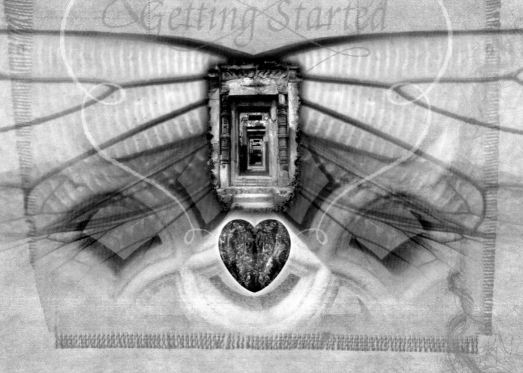

What does your heart say,

all by itself?

With no obligation to others,

no guilt,

no thought of "what will they think?"

Just you, and the rest

of the vast starry universe;

Not even God.

Just you, alone.

What does your heart say?

— RICHARD WEHRMAN

GETTING STARTED

Heartwork is a process of letting go, with awareness, into the truth of one's being in the moment. It is essentially a very simple process—kind of like falling asleep, except that in Heartwork, one falls awake—but it is not easy. It is simple because all you have to do is find the yearning in your being (to be free, whole, connected, alive; to know who and what you are; to realize what reality is—whatever form it takes for you) and let go or surrender into it and let it take you back home to your authentic, true self. It is difficult because letting go into unfamiliar places inside ourselves is scary. We are used to controlling our emotions, our lives, other people and anything else we think we need to control.

Why is it so scary? For a good reason. Most people think they're afraid of the unknown. Actually, that's not true because it's not possible to be afraid of the unknown. The unknown is unknown; it is not a thing that one can fear. What we are really afraid of is what we think we might encounter on our journey inward: our fear, anger, pain—everything that was too much for us to feel when it happened, so that we had to wall it off from our consciousness. That could include negative self-images and beliefs, aloneness, emptiness, nothingness, existential angst or even the much-talked-about dark night of the soul. And the truth is that we usually have to go through all of these to come home to ourselves.

Many people are afraid to make this journey because they believe that what is at the deepest level inside themselves is bad, some "original sin," and they don't want their belief to be confirmed. (I distinguish between "belief" and "faith" in that faith is based on direct, personal experience, whereas belief is merely a thought.) How could we live with ourselves if we knew that our true nature was really awful? So many of us don't ever look deeply enough to uncover the truth of who or what we really are, which is absolutely the antithesis of awful (but it is awe full!).

When I first began the deep feeling part of my journey, I started writing a book entitled *Cheap Insights*. I made all of one entry into the book: "I used to think that when I got through my fear that I would come to life. Then I realized that my life was in my fear!" By allowing myself to feel my fear completely, I lost my fear of being afraid and I began (after a few decades of emotional anesthesia) to allow myself to re-experience the full range of human emotions—fear, sadness, anger and *joy*! I began to come back to life in my feelings.

When we split our consciousness off from our feelings, we feel disconnected from ourselves, others, the universe and God. We cannot let love in or out; we cannot appreciate the exquisite beauty and awe of life. We feel, as A. E. Housman once suggested, alone and afraid in a world we never made.

So how then can we do the impossible—let go into the very places that so terrify us, the places we have separated ourselves from for decades? Actually, the way it usually happens is that the opportunity catches up with us—we don't have to go looking for it! For most people who do this challenging work, life has become unbearably painful, difficult and unsatisfying. And at that point, they have two options: either take the journey inward or medicate with prescription drugs or other addictions to deaden themselves. (This is not to say that psychopharmacologic medications are never appropriate and necessary for one's journey; but the reality is that we frequently use them as crutches to avoid our issues rather than as tools to support us in working with those issues).

Here's how it works. Picture a funnel. Our true nature is a single point at the bottom of the funnel, whole and undivided. We first split from this wholeness when we get the idea that we are a self that is separate from others and from the universe. We call this split the formation of the ego. I've been asked why we make this split in the first place. The only answer I've ever heard that's worth repeating came from my Zen teacher, who said we split from wholeness so that we can experience the joy of coming back home to ourselves! With the formation of the ego, we have moved one layer up the funnel away from our true nature.

With the ego come the notions of space and time. We perceive space because now we see an inside (the ego, or the "I") and an outside (the universe), whereas before it was all one thing. We perceive time because while the universe will seemingly go on forever, the self will not. And because it is untenable to live in the awareness of our ultimate demise, we split from ourselves once again and tell ourselves that while our bodies will die, our consciousness, our soul or our spirit (or who we convince ourselves we *really are*) will not—it will go on forever. And so we make another split as we separate our physical selves from our soul or our spirit and move up the funnel away from our true nature.

Now to make matters worse, certain parts of our mind or soul or spirit are unacceptable to our parents and our culture. I've come to understand that we have four fundamental emotions—joy/love, sorrow/pain, fear (the movement away from sorrow/pain) and anger (fear or pain projected outward because we are unwilling to feel those more vulnerable emotions). Of these, only joy/love is truly acceptable in society. (And actually, we only say it is; look at how we react to people exuberantly enjoying themselves!) But guess what happens to our joy when we cut off the other three feelings? It gets cut off, too, because you can't have real joy unless you accept pain. Is it any wonder that we see so few truly joyous human beings in our culture beyond the age of 2 or 3? We also judge as unacceptable certain desires (such as greed, lust and envy) and even certain out-of-the-ordinary states of awareness (such as ESP, intuition, channeling and psychosis).

And so we split again into what Carl Jung called the persona (those parts of ourselves that we believe are acceptable to our culture and that we are willing to express publicly) and the shadow (those parts we believe are unacceptable to others and that we consequently try to hide from the world as well as from ourselves). Now, the problem with the shadow is that it has to somehow find expression or life. After all, it is called the shadow because it sticks to us wherever we go, yet it remains hidden and dark. Because we won't let it breathe fresh air, so to speak, it sneaks out in some other way, unconsciously, hurting others and ourselves.

To make matters even worse, certain things happen to us as we are growing up (and "growing up" continues even when we're 80 and beyond) that are just too painful or too frightening to fully experience at the time. So we wall these experiences off in our unconscious mind, where we store those events and aspects of our being that we protect ourselves from experiencing. Thus we move one step further up the funnel to the point where we are living our lives—on the upper rim.

So that's the bad news. Here's the good news. For some of us, it becomes apparent at some point that we are suffering and cannot find a way out of it—not through drugs and alcohol, sex, money, power, success, religion or any of the other addictions or distractions with which we try to fill this nagging emptiness inside ourselves. The reason we get to this point is that our deepest yearning is to regain our lost wholeness and connectedness, and in its great wisdom, our unconscious mind repeatedly creates situations that remind us of the places where we originally split from ourselves. It does this not to punish us but to get our attention, so that we can stop running away from those parts of ourselves that we have split off from. If we are willing to face ourselves, we can then "take the hit" (feel those feelings we've repressed) and feel all the way back to where the original pain and fear occurred so we can heal the wound at its source. As my dear friend Cis Dickson has embroidered on the back of her Crooked Back Ranch caps, "Go Within or Go Without." When we get to this point in our lives, it is actually easier to let go into the yearning than to keep running away from the fear of facing what lies within ourselves. And so the journey homeward begins!

The purpose of this book is to share the essential tools, processes and understandings of Heartwork so that you may have a direct experience of healing your wounds at their source. It is my hope that by using Heartwork on a regular basis as a tool for personal transformation, you will bring peace, joy and love into your life—and by so doing, into the world.

The big question is whether you are going to be able to say a hearty "yes" to your adventure.

— JOSEPH CAMPBELL

PART II: A HEARTWORK EXPERIENCE

To maximize your experience of Heartwork, I highly recommend that you work through as much of this section of the book as possible in one sitting. This work is cumulative and tends to build upon itself, taking you increasingly deeper into your being. If you can, take a whole day or an entire weekend to ensure that you have enough time to spaciously explore the Heartwork process. You might also consider journaling your responses to each of the questions posed.

Light
Will someday split you open
Even if your life is now a cage.

Little by little,
You will turn into stars.

Little by little,
You will turn into
The whole sweet, amorous Universe.

Love will surely burst you wide open
Into an unfettered, booming new galaxy.

You will become so free
In a wonderful, secret
And pure Love
That flows
From a conscious,
One-pointed,
Infinite Light.

Even then, my dear,
The Beloved will have fulfilled
Just a fraction,
Just a fraction!
Of a promise
He wrote upon your heart.

For a divine seed, the crown of destiny,
Is hidden and sown on an ancient, fertile plain
You hold the title to.

O look again within yourself,
For I know you were once the elegant host
To all the marvels in creation.

When your soul begins
To ever bloom and laugh
And spin in Eternal Ecstasy —

O little by little,
You will turn into God.

—HAFIZ

Something wants
to dance out of these words,
to sing a song of praise and thanksgiving.

A voice like the first birds,
calling into the blackgrey suncoming morning

With no particular words to say
or to understand —
just chirping like sizzling popcorn,
water into oil

Dancing on the fire,
feet flying from the flames
but loving it:

these amazing acrobatics
I never knew that I could do,
singing my heart out,
perfectly still

An arrow arcing into dawn,
released to the pull of my own heartwood,
driving deep

Into the clear morning air,
splitting love's arrow already in my chest,
humming and vibrating still.

—RICHARD WEHRMAN

ORIENTATION

We do not see things as they are, we see things as we are.

—TALMUDIC SAYING

....

THE ESSENTIAL ORIENTATION OF HEARTWORK IS:

B e curious about whatever arises in each moment, asking nonjudgmentally, "What is this?" and be open and vulnerable to whatever is there. In other words, be willing to "take the hit" and to fully experience what opens in your awareness.

S urrender into your deepest yearning for awakening, realization (of self, true nature, ultimate truth, reality), freedom, aliveness or wholeness—and then let that yearning take you home.

....

The processes you will be invited to practice in this book
will give you an experiential understanding
of these two statements.

All fear,
all revelation,
all beauty and amazement,
arise from your own Mind.

You are the source of it all.

You stare at vaporous
black squiggles upon a white page,
and insight arises.

From where?

You hear a cacophony of sounds,
no different than wind in the trees,
or leaves tumbling over the ground,
and you bow in gratitude
to your teacher.

Where is this teacher?

You think it all comes from somewhere else.

Listen!
Where is it all actually occurring?

I don't mean to sound angry —
but this is Me, shaking You:

Right now
these tumbling letters
are rattling around inside your head
and you think
it's me talking to you,
when really it is your own Mystery —

Alive and fully Present,
creating me, these words,
and everything else you see.

Wake up!
See this one who reads,
this one who writes.

In this search
of a thousand years,
we've freed the usual suspects —
and as unlikely as it seemed
in the beginning,

You are the only One left.

—RICHARD WEHRMAN

WHAT DO YOU WANT?

Life is suffering" is one translation of the first of the Buddha's Four Noble Truths. We are all suffering. We all want things we don't have and we all have things we don't want. This is the cause of our suffering.

So if this is the simple truth, why can't we end our suffering by fully concurring with our lives—having what we have and wanting nothing more or less?

Believe it or not, the answer is that we have lost touch with what we really want and have substituted a whole lot of other things for that for which we most deeply yearn. We go around thinking that if only we had enough money, sex, power, fame, drugs and alcohol, or knowledge, we would finally be happy. But no amount of these things will satisfy us because none of them is what we really want. (That you are now reading this book indicates that you have already figured this out!) The more of these things we get, the more we want, and so we can never be fully satisfied. As long as we think those things are what we want, we can never find the peace and fulfillment we are longing for.

One reason none of these things brings us happiness is that they all are focused on the future. They are all predicated on attaining something that we don't already have. And happiness can only happen *now*, in this very moment. We cannot be happy in the future because the future will always be just a thought we are having right now! And as long as we are focused on achieving something greater in the future which will finally satisfy our longing, we can never be truly happy.

But the main reason none of these things brings us peace and happiness is that they're not what we really hunger for. What we really long for is our true selves—our wholeness and our connectedness with others and with the universe or God. And the truth is that we already have these things because they are innate; we don't have to go searching for them outside ourselves. The problem is that we don't know—or actually, that we have forgotten—that we already have these treasures and that we already are whole and complete and connected to all life.

So, how then do we remember that and wake up to the truth of ourselves? This book has been written to help you find your way back home to yourself, to take you on that journey of self re-membering—to reclaim the truth you have forgotten.

Seek the truth…
and the truth shall set you free…

but what is this truth of which I speak?…
it is not factual…
although you must strive,
scrupulously,
and relentlessly,
for subjective honesty…

it is not knowledge or wisdom…
although you will acquire both
along the way…

it is not a philosophy or a religion…
although it is profoundly spiritual,
and you will develop a personal ethic
of great power and substance…

but rather it is a state of being,
where, suddenly,
self-deception is swept away…
and you are left with the essence
of who you really are…

in that moment,
you are filled with power and glory,
and you are at one with the universe…

all fear and judgment disappear…
and what remains
is strength,
beauty,
and joy…
empathy
and compassion…
understanding
and acceptance…
and unconditional love
for all of creation…
and you will forever long to return
to this wondrous place.

— CAROL SWIEDLER

The journey begins with acknowledging the suffering and dissatisfaction in your life. What is not working? What do you want that you don't have? Is it a love relationship, your health, enough money, peace of mind, a feeling of aliveness or joy, a sense of wholeness or connectedness? And what do you have that you don't want? Where exactly are you on the surface of the funnel of your life? Wherever you are, that is your doorway to your inner journey home to yourself.

The following exercise will guide you through the first Heartwork process offered in this book. You may journal or contemplate your answers—whatever works best for you. What is most important is that you become fully engaged in the process. As with everything in life, you get out of it exactly what you put into it. If you give little of yourself to the process, you'll get little back. If you give a lot, you'll get a lot back. And if you give all of yourself to the process, you'll get all of yourself out of it!

PLEASE PROCEED ONE PAGE AT A TIME WITHOUT
LOOKING AHEAD.

The process is sequential,
and knowing what comes next
will defeat the purpose
of the exercise.

So, to begin, I'd like to ask you a question,

and I invite you to give it thorough and serious consideration before you answer. It is absolutely vital that you answer truthfully—from where you actually live your life, rather than from where you would like to live it. And, again, please do not turn the page until you're done. Now, with all that said,

What do you want?

What do you want?

What do   you want?

What do   you want?

Now let me reshape that question a little.

And once again, I invite you to
consider your answer thoroughly
and seriously:

What do you want that you don't have?

What do you want that you don't have?

And now the other side of the coin:

What do you have that you don't want?

What do you have that you don't want?

Now I want to challenge you with a statement that I believe is usually true. The first time I heard this I didn't want to accept it. But the more I have thought about and worked with it, the more I see the truth in it:

If you want to know what you really want, look at what you have. What you have is what you really want!

What does this mean? It means that, despite what we tell ourselves about what we want, we always get what we really want. We are essentially run by our unconscious desires, motives, wants and needs. Our actions speak louder than our words! At least 51 percent of each of us wants what we have, or else we would have something else. Just think about it. It must be true! Even with things that are hereditary or seemingly forced upon us, we *choose* how we want to relate to them. For example, I say—and believe—that I want to lose weight, but I keep overeating. Obviously, for some unconscious reason, I don't really want to lose weight. If I did, I would stop overeating. The same is true for all addictions (anything we do repetitively to avoid dealing with discomfort)—we say we're going to quit, but we never do. We really want to hold onto this behavior for some reason that we don't yet understand.

So before we can change our lives, we must wake up to what is running us unconsciously—we must become conscious of these unconscious wants and needs and of the belief systems fashioned in our formative years. Only then can we come to understand why we do what we do and have what we have.

We are constantly creating our own reality, our own world. (Even in this moment, you are creating a reality out of the words you are reading here.) And until we take full responsibility for what we have created, we cannot change our lives. We will remain a victim of circumstances, continually blaming them and other people for our fate. So despite what you tell yourself about what you want, what is the real truth?

What do you really want?

If you want to know what you REALLY want,
look at what you have.

What you have
is what you
REALLY
want!

What do you really want?

What do you really want?

There's a very good reason why we create what we have. As I explained earlier, we split from our true nature in an effort to protect ourselves from feelings and events that are too painful or frightening to deal with at the time. We wall off these events in our unconscious and create beliefs about who we are and what the world is about. And out of these unconscious beliefs we then create a world—our world—that perpetuates our suffering. (For example, when children are emotionally or physically abused and/or abandoned, they do not yet have the cognitive capacity to deal with such immense pain. They create the belief that the parent is unable to be loving and present because something is wrong or lacking in the child. "I'm not good enough for Mommy to love me," the child thinks, "but if I'm better behaved, then Mommy will love me." This "I'm not good enough" belief carries over into adulthood and gets played out in future relationships, creating untold suffering and dissatisfaction. In fact, that belief runs the person's life, creating the same kind of suffering over and over.)

That's the bad news. The good news is that the deepest yearning in all of us is to return home to our true nature—to wholeness, love, freedom, joy and happiness. And our unconscious mind, in its absolute brilliance, repeatedly creates the precise situations we need in order to feel our long-buried pain so that we can heal it at its source. We need only to stop running away from ourselves, accept that we have created what we've created, and then look and *feel* into the painful circumstances of our lives so we can heal that split within ourselves and so open into wholeness.

So now, most importantly:

Why do you want what you have?

Take your time with this question. Look and feel as deeply as you possibly can into it—see and feel exactly where the belief that you're living was formed.

Why do you want what you have?

Now that you've seen what your unconscious mind wants—
what's been running the show all this time—let me ask you
one more time:

Underneath everything,
what do you really, really want?

Can you feel where this deep yearning lives in your body?

Underneath everything, what do you really, really want?

*S*o...

*What's in the way of your
having what you really, really want?*

What's in between your yearning and where you live your life? Please look
into this question as deeply as possible because you can't have what you
really, really want until you see what's in the way of your having it.

What's in the way of your having what you really, really want?

*A*nd...

What do you have to do to get through
or beyond what's in the way of your having
what you really, really want?

What do you have to do to get through or beyond what's in the way of your having what you really, really want?

What are you waiting for?

The tragedy of life is not so much what people suffer,
but rather what they miss.

—THOMAS CARLYLE

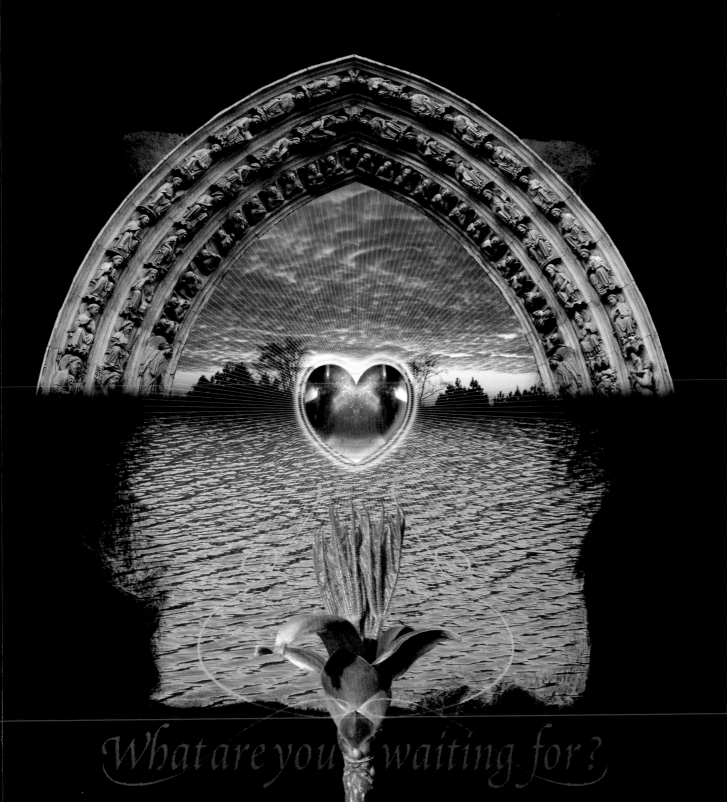

What are you waiting for?

Now what?...

We are sailors
on a strange dark sea,
Shoving our boarded boats
from shore and sand
into riotous nights
of wind and crashing
thunder.

When all sane men
(could we but be)
at home well covered
in dry warm
beds lie lee.

But here our driven-ness
and our call,
all soaked and thrown and tossed—
Tumbling,
brothered by fear,
lamped by longing—

Find we are

Rowing,
rowing fiercely
towards the darkest center
of the storm.

— RICHARD WEHRMAN

NOW WHAT?

In answering the questions in the "What Do You Want?" exercise, could you *feel* the sense of dissatisfaction—right where it lives within your body/mind? Where in your body did you experience the discomfort, ache or blockage?

What did it feel like?

And how did you then—and how do you now—relate to this uncomfortable sensation? Do you hate it, ignore it, push it away, fight it? Or do you move towards it, into it, embrace it, want to know and understand it?

There's a saying that I often use, "The only way out is through." Paradoxically, whatever you are looking for in life—whatever the source of your dissatisfaction and suffering may be—it can be found right in the center of the very thing you are avoiding within yourself.

So I'd like to invite you to end the fight within and against yourself and begin the journey homeward—the yellow brick road back home to your true nature—by allowing yourself to begin to move toward this aching and yearning that you have just come into contact with. In truth, the journey back to your true self is accomplished by making direct contact with this inner longing and then simply (but not necessarily easily) surrendering or letting go—with awareness—into the yearning itself.

The journey requires patience, perseverance, determination, courage, self-forgiveness and compassion, discriminating wisdom, willingness, vulnerability, intuition, power and strength—all qualities that paradoxically are further developed in the process of undertaking the journey.

How do we become so emotionally dead that we create all the pain we've created for both ourselves and for others? And how can we come back to the life within us so that we can stop creating all this suffering in the world?

Here is how I understand it:

As I previously explained, when we split from our true nature (our wholeness, joy, peace or love), we create an untenable existential angst or despair. The deepest pain we will ever experience is the pain of separating from ourselves. Think of it as falling out of Paradise (our own Garden of Eden). After this come innumerable other painful experiences that are simply too much for us to process. Moving away from this pain creates fear—fear of feeling the pain that has now become trapped inside us, and fear of experiencing yet more pain in the future. When we split from fear, we usually move into anger, which is really one's pain projected outward, often onto another. And because anger is not generally acceptable in this culture, we move into numbness and emotional deadness. And this is where most people spend the vast majority of their lives.

As in all forms of natural healing, the journey home to our true self usually requires a retracing process—working our way, often step by step (but not necessarily in any particular order), back through the layers of suppression. This often means that a person will start by waking up to the awareness that something is not really right with his or her life. The person feels a growing sense of dissatisfaction and frustration. Eventually the frustration evolves into anger. Sometimes the anger becomes great enough that it causes major problems—like losing a job or a relationship. Or there may be the threat—explicit or intuited—of such a loss. Or the anger may be turned against oneself and manifest as depression. At this point, some people will seek help. Unfortunately, most "helpers" seek only to ameliorate the symptoms and never attempt to find the source of the dissatisfaction, where the only true and lasting healing can take place.

If, however, the person is fortunate enough to find a helper who understands the process of deep healing, he or she will be encouraged to gently open into the anger, to see and feel what is underneath or behind it. What's immediately under the surface of anger is fear. There is really just one fear—the archetypal Fear created by our separation from our true nature—but that Fear becomes attached to many external situations and becomes any number of other smaller fears.

When you can open deeply into those smaller fears, you can feel the pain underneath them and you finally see The Fear. And when you open fully into The Fear, you experience The Pain (of splitting from yourself). This opens you to the deep angst or despair that's often referred to as the dark night of the soul, which is the doorway back home to yourself.

These stages come up in a very natural unfolding process—each in its own way and time—when you allow yourself to surrender to your deepest yearning. The yearning actually comes from your true nature or wholeness, and it takes you back to your undivided true self. All you have to do is get out of your own way, let go, stay present, and let the yearning do all the work for you.

That said, transformational work is, of course, an individual matter from beginning to end. Though people may have issues and experiences in common, each person comes to the work with a unique situation, with specific wishes for increased well-being and with his or her own (yet-to-be-discovered) natural healing process.

Because of that, there's no one way or even preferred way to do Heartwork. Yet sometimes people find it helpful to have some idea of where this work may take them and what its potentials are for personal growth. With that in mind, here's a general overview of how the process generally unfolds:

1. Acknowledge that you have a problem, or that something is missing in your life, and get clear on what that is.

2. Take responsibility for changing your life. Become willing and committed to doing whatever it takes to free yourself from suffering.

3. With the issues of your life as a focus, learn and put into practice your inner working process.

4. Go through the "swamp" and glimpse freedom.

5. Develop your own process through experience, determination, patience and confidence.

6. Open to new awareness of who you are and what life is all about.

7. Integrate your insights into your everyday life.

In the course of your work, a number of deep issues may surface that will need resolution. You may:

1. Begin to really *feel*: open fully to love, joy, sorrow, fear and anger. In the process of socialization, we are taught to suppress our feelings. We become cut off from our feeling nature and often become emotionally paralyzed or dead. In the process of re-accessing our feelings, we need to go through a phase of learning how to express our long-buried emotions. Ultimately, however, when we have created a powerful enough foundation of awareness, we become able to "impress," rather than suppress or express our feelings. In other words, we can allow ourselves to fully experience the emotion in the moment—by allowing it to energize our life, by inquiring into it as it is happening and by experiencing the transformation of what we usually think of as a negative emotion into a more positive emotion (for example, anger becoming power, fear becoming love and compassion, sorrow and pain becoming beauty and awe).

2. Reclaim or heal (love, embrace, accept) your inner child: make contact with all parts of the inner child, see the predicaments clearly, allow any unfelt or unacknowledged feelings to surface, and allow the child to finally get what he or she needs (from yourself, primarily, and then from others).

3. Make peace with your parents: see or feel your parents as they are and/or were, and experience your own related feelings; forgiving your parents and yourself for all the mutual creation of pain; mourn the loss of the perfect, unconditionally loving parents you never had; and, ultimately, become your own wished-for parents and reparent yourself.

4.   Recognize, claim and balance within yourself the masculine and feminine energies.

5.   Open to the animal and elemental aspects of humanness and reconnect with the natural world.

6.   Claim your deepest resources (your gifts to the world) and accept, with lightness, your "foolishness."

7.   In relationship, become capable of loving and being loved and be open to seeing, feeling and communicating clearly with both yourself and others.

8.   Do transpersonal work: see that you are more than bodily sensations, thoughts and feelings and open to your innate qualities (including awareness, curiosity, love and compassion, wisdom and discrimination, intuition, inspiration and vision, will and willpower, courage, determination, vulnerability, willingness to risk, authenticity, spontaneity and creativity, passion, forgiveness, joy, peace and faith in yourself and in God or the universe).

9.   Do work of a spiritual nature: learn to live in a state of questioning or not-knowing or being; experience your fundamental separation (aloneness, emptiness, nothingness) and open to and move through despair into a state of oneness (undivided and interconnected with all life); facing death (of the ego or "I", the known), and come to know your true self.

10. Live responsibly from a place of openness, honesty, integrity and commitment to creating wholeness in yourself, others and the world. Just as in the emotional maturational process of moving from suppressing emotions to expressing and ultimately impressing them, in this stage we grow from being dependent on others to becoming independent and ultimately to realizing our interdependence with all existence.

Along the way, you see clearly that suffering is created by resistance to pain and that the way out is *in*. By opening into and moving through your blocks, layer after layer, you enter into increasingly open, and decreasingly painful, states of being. Seeing this, you naturally move toward difficulty rather than away from it, and you gradually come to trust your ability to work through any problem that may arise. Life then becomes an adventure to be lived and learned from.

While you ultimately have to do the work for yourself, it is often helpful to work with someone who has "gone before" and who can provide guidance, support and encouragement on the journey. At some point, you outgrow the need to work with a Heartwork facilitator. Although you may at times need assistance in looking into a particularly difficult issue, for the most part you have truly "graduated" and are empowered to create a full and satisfying life.

Happiness consists in finding out precisely what the "one thing necessary" may be in our lives, and in gladly relinquishing all the rest. For then, by a divine paradox, we find that everything else is given us together with the one thing we needed.

—THOMAS MERTON

There is nothing but water in the holy pools.
    I know, I have been swimming in them.

All the gods sculpted of wood or ivory can't say a word.
    I know, I have been crying out to them.

The sacred Books of the East are nothing but words.
    I looked through their covers one day sideways.

What Kabir talks of is only what he has lived through.

If you have not lived through something, it is not true.

—KABIR

Compass
for finding your way home...

Telescope
for seeing clearly what used to deceive you...

Rope
to keep you safe on the way down...

PickAxe
for breaking up the bedrock of your past...

Drill
to penetrate persistant fears...

Shovel
to remove the manure you've been standing in...

Crowbar
to pry loose whatever stands in your way...

Wrench
to remove the rusty bolts from your Heart...

TOOLS FOR INNER WORK

Who so desires the ocean makes light of streams.

—AHMED 'IBN-AL-'HUSAYN AL-'MUTANABDI

What follows are a number of options for proceeding further—if you're willing. Each of the Heartwork processes I describe in this section gives you an opportunity to go all the way into and through the barriers you have created that prevent you from having the life you really, really want. Find the ones that work best for you. But feel free to come back to the others occasionally to see if they might speak more loudly to you in the future.

First-person accounts written by workshop participants and those who have done Heartwork in individual private sessions follow the description of each tool and appear in italics. An asterisk (*) placed after a contributor's name indicates that the name used is a pseudonym. The experiences people have had using these tools are as varied as the number of people who have used them, and your experience will likewise be uniquely your own. These heartfelt accounts, however, will give you some idea of how meaningful these tools can be in enriching your process and deepening your inner journey.

Warning: The exercises in this section are designed to help you open your awareness to, and reclaim aspects of, your being that you may have split yourself off from. This opening and reclaiming will enable you to have more access to the full range of human experience. Some of the processes can be emotionally disturbing and painful. If you are currently seeing a mental health professional for psychological or emotional conditions, consult that professional before attempting any of the exercises in this section. If you experience any moderate or severe emotional discomfort in practicing any of these exercises, it is strongly advised that you seek professional guidance from a mental health practitioner before continuing the exercise.

A Simple Death

Secret sorrows of this heart
The truth of my body received
Each cell a journal, pages filled
With experience left to retrieve

And I, the coward, warrior, fool
To hold the only key
Which unlocks all the tendril paths
To my divinity

How deep and bloodied were the ways
I struggled to believe
When now the only solace, a simple death
Is the truth of my body received

Its course uncharted sings me home
I have only to concede
My fear and anguish, trust and follow
The truth of my body to be freed.

—HALLIE SAWYERS

UNWINDING

Within this fathomlong body is found all the teachings, is found suffering,
the cause of suffering, and the end of suffering.

—BUDDHA

Unwinding is what your cat or dog does when it has too much tension in its body. Pets stretch, growl, snarl, meow—whatever they need to do to release the tension they are holding—and all unselfconsciously. We, too, inhabit animal bodies that know what they need to do to release tension. All you have to do is to get out of the way and allow your body to let go: stretch, moan, groan, cry, wail, scream, shout, yawn. Unwinding is a skill that needs to be relearned. We knew how to do it when we were little, but as we got older we outgrew it (we were told, in one way or another, that it was unacceptable behavior). The CD that comes with the book contains two pieces of music composed specifically for Unwinding by Todd Carter. So put them on, simply feel into your deepest yearning (what you really, really want), and just give your body permission to let go. This relearning may take some practice, but it is well worth it.

My body knows how. All I have to do is just stay with myself; stay with the organic process of what is unwinding out of me. But I sour overnight like milk left out and forgotten. I wake in the dark and a feeling of being utterly lost and alone engulfs every cell. I stave it off and try to slip back into sleep. So the feeling builds and waits for me. There is a moment each morning before I open my eyes when it strikes at every facet of the tendermost me. I come to consciousness writhing and twisting away from this familiar pain.

I lie to myself about it. Not so hard. Not so bad. Not so awful. And so I get up laying lie upon lie over this fire burning in my gut, in my heart, in my soul. Hoping to extinguish it. Bargaining at least to deaden it. Knowing. Knowing the quicksilver pulse of my life beats deep within this pain and unwilling to brave the flames to save myself.

I see my feet in wool socks crossing the kitchen floor. I hear the faraway sound they make from my perch atop the pillar of lies I use to stamp out this fire. I eat. I drink. Everything goes into my mouth with an eye toward killing this pain. Then the pain, not to be outdone, emits a siren call, ransacking the stored emotion inscribed in each cell of my body for reinforcement. And my thoughts turn unbidden to specific hardship.

Always something I've done to irrevocably hurt. Carved in ready detail, this hurt pushes to the surface of my consciousness to feed the painfire.

I turn from it, averting my eyes from the catastrophe of me. "I'll get back to ya." "Perhaps another time." The liar bargaining her way out of conversation, out of the hearts of those she loves the most in order to avoid the emptiness consuming her.

Yet this pain is patient. It abides. And something in the way that it waits cuts through all the armor I've built to shield myself. It waits for me like no one has ever waited. Honor-bound to see me through, it waits for me like I long to be waited for.

The longing becomes the edge that splits me open to this pain. I let it have me. Finding the floor. Falling. Rending. Splitting from all that I know, an eerie sound is born deep inside this vortex—my own voice, honed by a lifetime of longing, keening the loss of me. Wolves calling the moon.

Unwinding with this sound comes the familiar face of my longing: the victim. And this time I am not her. I see that no crevice of her pain has gone unplumbed. She's worn out from the ways I've used her, prostituted her pain for an answer to this longing. She wails, "You'll never stop!" and the man I've blamed all my life for this pain appears.

I see my father from the back. He turns and wears my own face. I am this, too. I know now. I AM THIS, TOO. The boundary of my skin won't contain me anymore, won't contain this revelation. My mouth stretches to howl unspeakable words. In my voice is a self unfurling itself; sound birthing me home into the heart of the need that rules me. The need that owns me. The need that feeds the pain of both abuser and abused.

Its tide rips out the timeworn markers of all the falsehoods I've used to hold it back: Healer in the name of solving my own pain; giver in the name of filling my own need; liar in the name of protecting the emptiness that steers everything I do. I let the unsolvable mystery at the heart of this pain claim me. I hear my voice, only vowel-round: IYEEE…IYEEE…IYEEE. I NEED…I NEED…I NEED.

All I know is need. I am need embodied. In this single moment I see across the ocean of time and choice that have come together, bringing me here, midwife to the need I can no longer hold back; mother to the orphaned child alive within me; owner of the first hurt and author of all the rest.

Shining, whole, honor-bound, somewhere from the depths of me comes my pain transformed. In bearing the depth of my own anguish is born another self. Within my hands, my arms, within all of who I am there is a solace that would cradle the world. I see my truth in liar's rags and love the broken-whole of me. I am gathered in my own arms. The need I thought would kill me is answered and I sleep.

—ELIZABETH SOTO*

I see Unwinding as a journey that I have forgotten but my body has not. I use this exercise to tune into my body's wisdom, turning down the noise in my mind so I don't hear its chatter and my body is better able to communicate with me. My eyes close, my body moves and does whatever it wants. At some point, I experience a knowing, and my body unfolds its wisdom.

I had a particularly extraordinary spiritual experience with Unwinding one morning at a Heartwork seminar. The Unwinding started my process of seeing all that I AM. I asked God that I may see from my eyes and not just feel and know. God replied that I see from my soul. Knowing this was the truth, and knowing that I am the truth, I started to cry.

This knowingness intensified in my heart and soul, and in that moment my son's spirit spoke to me from that place. "Mommy, remember who you are," he said. "I know who you are." My son then took me by the hand and touched my heart and soul through the truth of his soul. Wisdom came. He then said, "Let everyone know here that words are very powerful and whatever you say and do to the children, we feel it to the core of our being: good or bad—so remember."

I recalled doing some earlier work when I learned that the part of me who is a defiant angry child would not allow me to take in the love and abundance that God gives so freely. I felt so unsafe while I was growing up and the knowing I had at that time was so scary that I stopped remembering who I was. It wasn't safe then, I realized, but it is now.

I continued to unwind into my heart and soul, with my son teaching me to remember through his heart and soul and to accept this with great joy and love. I accepted who I was and that I was free to be all that I came here to be. This knowing filled my entire being, and as I felt the presence of God's love, my son said, "I will always be in your heart, Mommy." He kissed my heart and soul with the love God gave him to give.

I allowed this to fill my entire being, and it's still there. I take it in whenever I am in need of it. My son will be going off to college in the next few months, and I am so grateful that I have that special moment that will last for a lifetime. After this meditation experience, I can let go and let my son live the life that he came here to live. I can do this with no controlling, just allowing the will of God to take care of all his needs—and mine at the same time.

—MARGIE MENSIK

Beloved,
presence of being,
every sound

the call of your voice;
every sight,
the beauty of your

incomparable body,
Every touch, every breeze, every blow
your caress upon my hand.

All of you, here.
Giving yourself completely, absolutely.

Arm in arm,
the mirror and the merged,
together we sip

the deep red honey wine of union,
only to discover –
we have wed not only each other

but the whole wide world.

—RICHARD WEHRMAN

SOFT BODY MEDITATION

The Soft Body Meditation (which you will find on track 4 of the Heartwork CD) dissolves the sense of a separate self by opening you to your inherent vulnerability. As we grow up we learn to wall off experiences from our consciousness that are too painful to deal with, thinking that if we can keep them behind a strong barricade we will never have to feel them. But this is just wishful thinking. The truth is that when we wall things off from our consciousness, we don't really lock them out—we lock them in! They eat away at us from the inside until something eventually breaks (and in this culture, it's usually our bodies). The only true invulnerability is total vulnerability! If we are willing to completely experience the pain or fear created by life's inevitabilities, we don't get stuck anywhere. We can then feel them fully and let go of them. There is no residue, no accumulation of tension-creating, dis-ease-producing toxic emotional baggage. The Soft Body Meditation allows us to open the body gently and gradually, to allow the armoring to dissolve and the heart and mind to open.

> *Please note:* When working with the experiential exercises that are included on the CD that accompanies this book, it is best to keep one finger on the "Play" and "Pause" buttons on your CD player or your remote control so that you can determine the pace at which you go through the steps of the exercises.

I have been an anxious person for as long as I can remember. My anxiety affects every aspect of my life, and I am always reminded of its presence. Oddly enough, in the present moment, I am not anxious—I am only anxious once I think about what could happen, even if it's improbable. So staying in the present moment has become valuable to me, and I use the Soft Body meditation to help me do this.

The first time I tried Soft Body, I could feel my thoughts resisting. As a person who has a hard time staying present, I also have a hard time keeping still. In really focusing on my body and giving it the time and energy it deserves, I realized this was something I had not yet done in my life. My body had been sorely neglected! Sure, I had tended to headaches and similar pains, but when the body is really aching in this way, it means we have ignored it far too long. I had to concentrate on clearing my mind of any thoughts other than receiving the sensations my body was experiencing in each moment. Immediately, I realized that not only was I experiencing a different sensation in every moment, but that in order to fully experience each sensation, I had to let go of the previous sensation. The experience I remember most clearly was this one:

I am lying down, giving full attention to my body and all the energy and sensations within it. I start with the top of my head and listen to hear if that part of my body is trying to tell me something. I am not listening with my ears; I am listening with a part of my conscious self that is deeper than the part whose thoughts easily wander. I pay full attention to what the top of my head is feeling, and I notice that it itches. I don't reach up to scratch it, but I focus on the itch in the moment and give it the attention it needs. Within moments the feeling disappears and I am ready to move on down my body.

I go from body part to body part, letting go completely of the previous part and giving my total attention to the part I am currently focusing on. As I sweep down my body, I notice different sensations: itchiness, tingling, a feeling of heaviness, a feeling of lightness. I concentrate on each sensation and then let go of it. When I arrive at my lower abdomen, I start to experience pain. I begin to sense that most of my anxiety resides in this part of my body and it will require more time.

As I focus on the physical pain, I slowly begin to experience emotional pain. Concentrating on the emotional pain, I sense that what I am feeling is not pain at all— it is fear. I cannot describe this fear. I do not try at this point to analyze what the fear is or where it comes from. All I am aware of at the moment is that a fear resides in this place within me and I have to find some way to let it go because I have no reason to hold onto it. I start to let out a sound, which gets l   and louder as I "exhale" the fear from my body. The pain begins to subside, and when it is gone, I find myself laughing uncontrollably.

Looking back, I think I was laughing because of the relief I felt in being able to let go of the fear in such a powerful way. I learned that day that our emotions find places in our bodies to live, and that they have a way of taking over our bodies if we let them. As a whole, we are more powerful than the emotions that reside in us. We can manifest peace within ourselves, but only when we feel our emotions in the present moment—and then let them go.

—ARIANE BAER

In the Soft Body meditation, my whole body opens to possibility. Answers come for me in the form of heightened full-body physical perceptions. They are like trips into sacred metaphors, and they are real. After the second Heartwork event I attended, while camping by myself, I did Soft Body in my tent every day. I became much more able to sense my surroundings, feeling no separation between me and the sounds of the birds and the wind. In one meditation, I could feel the breeze blow right through me. I could feel every single tiny bone in my hands and feet, as if I were a bird. I could sense the interconnectedness of my bones and my breath, my organs and my flesh.

When I practiced Soft Body in an "I and Thou" Heartwork retreat, I had visions that were incredibly healing for my sense of myself as a woman and my empowerment as a female. As I softened into the sensations of my body, I became a mother wolf, fangs and all. I was a life-giving nurturer but also a fierce protectress.

As I traveled down my body, I felt a powerful, grounding energy growing around me, like vines and tree roots taking hold. Vines wrapped me—not in a threatening way, but as if they were holding me securely. And then a tree-like arm, like the arm of God, began to grow through me. With this upward, surging will to live and to connect with the sky, the arm entered at the base of my spine, grew the length of my vertebrae, through my chest, through my throat and mouth and then, with strong but kind root-like fingers, it reached out through my mouth and embraced my face, cradling it.

I practice a form of yoga that channels energy up the spine using a series of energy loops. With Soft Body, I can feel that channel and the interconnectedness of all the energy loops more profoundly than I had ever felt them before. Soft Body also helped me feel space in my torso in places that I've typically had a hard time breathing into because of my scoliosis (a curvature of the spine). I am now bringing more breath to more of my rib cage, front and back. My spine seems to be following the force of the upward thrust of the root, organically unwinding, untwisting, opening. Because I feel my face is cradled, I open up to feeling the whole back of my skull more, and I can breathe more into the back of my body. When I am tuned into this arm/root meditation, it is impossible for me to abandon myself or to unconsciously evaluate myself from the outside. I am at home. I am moving with prana (vital life force)! It's amazing!

—KIRSCHE DICKSON

You will not exhaust
the love in the universe
if you were to absorb it
from now until the end of time.

Love is all that exists.

Love is the universal communication.
It is the energy that has created the
universe and is keeping it going.
God is Love.

All matter is formed by love.
There is an organic love
that speaks to everyone
if they could but hear.
A leaf holds together for love.

Love can turn the world around
and it does.
What did you think was spinning your planet
if it wasn't love
and what do you think the fires of your sun consist of
and the cells of your body
and the stars in your sky
and the consciousness in your heart?
It is all love.

There is nothing but love.
Don't let the masks and postures fool you.
Love is the glue
that holds the Universe together.
The greatest need in a soul
is to achieve that loving of self
which will bring about the unity
wherein the judgments
that have caused such pain
are eliminated.

—EMMANUEL'S BOOK

JUST LISTENING

Perhaps the greatest, most healing gift we can give each other is unconditional presence. One way of working with the emotional material that is released through the previous exercises is a tool called "Just Listening." This exercise creates a spiritual and emotional environment wherein one person can unburden his or her soul in the sacred space provided by the other's love and compassionate listening. It is one of the best tools I know for opening to and moving through the deep emotional material that prevents you from having what you really, really want. If used regularly (at least weekly), it will transform your life.

As with the previous exercises, Just Listening is fundamentally a very simple tool. At the same time, it is usually the tool most people have the most difficulty in really getting. It is best by far to practice it with a partner, but you can also do it alone. The goal of Just Listening is simply to let go as deeply as possible into your feelings around whatever issue has come up. While the technique is very simple and straightforward, it is very easy to get sidetracked by expressing thoughts about the issue instead of feelings. This is where most people go "wrong" in using this tool. It often takes people a number of tries before they master this exercise. The instructions below are for doing Just Listening with a partner.

1. Physically create a sacred space (one that feels comfortable, safe and private) and set aside at least four hours so the two of you can be completely undisturbed.

2. Partner A lies down (experiment with the position that allows for the greatest ease of opening). Partner B sits next to Partner A, without touching or looking at A, unless A requests it.

3. Partner A expresses any and all feelings that need to come out, not holding back anything, regardless of content or intensity. Partner A allows this releasing process to unfold until he or she feels absolutely complete.

4. During this process, Partner B just listens. Just listening means hearing Partner A's words and feeling the feelings along with A. If A is expressing difficult feelings toward or about B, then B listens as if A was talking about someone else and is just there for A. B does not spend even one second preparing a defense or a rebuttal of A's expression of feelings. *This exercise is absolutely not about being right.* It is about getting to the heart of the matter (the long suppressed feelings and the beliefs that formed out of them) for each individual. Partner B provides the safety of a compassionate external witness to allow Partner A to explore the uncharted and oftentimes frightening territory within. The only time B may say anything during this time is to remind A that he or she is exploring feelings, not thoughts.

One possible way this can be accomplished is for B to gently say to A, "That's a thought, not a feeling. What are you feeling?" This is the only thing B may say to A, uninvited. B may also not touch or even look at A unless invited to do so by A. This ensures that A's space will not be violated and makes it safe for A to get as vulnerable as possible in order to go all the way into his or her feelings.

5. When partner A is done, A and B switch places and roles. Partner B now has an opportunity to explore and express his or her feelings.

6. When Partner B feels complete, A may have another turn.

7. When A is done, B may have a second turn.

8. This going back and forth between A and B continues until both feel satisfied that they have done all they can do for this time.

The Just Listening exercise we learned at the "I and Thou" retreat this weekend was absolutely amazing. I found that after almost seven years with my partner, I actually heard him for the first time. The exercise was to just listen to my partner for ten minutes without facial expressions or feedback of any kind. As I sat and listened to him describe an argument we recently had, I was initially desperate to refute the things he was saying and defend myself against what I perceived to be an attack on something I had said that was, in my mind, "obviously" misinterpreted. I was angry and kept having to come back into presence and remind myself that I was there to listen and hear rather than interrupt and attack. As I continued to listen to him recount the argument, I began to soften and open. I was able to actually hear the words he was saying and feel how they affected him. By being present, my ego wasn't in control and therefore I didn't feel the need to belie the words being said. I could actually hear his truth about what had happened. When the ten minutes was over, I was able to respond with kindness and love to a situation that had previously been caustic and inflammatory. We were able to see for the first time how we repeatedly transform into five-year-old children when we have a disagreement. The exercise was so revealing. It really helped me feel connected to my partner in a way I truly never have before. We've committed to using this wonderfully powerful tool weekly to continue the work we did at the retreat. This has literally changed our lives.   —TRACI NOGE

In the Just Listening exercise, I decided to look into feelings of anger that I had toward my son for sexually violating my daughter, his half-sister, who was not quite three years old at the time. The incident had happened about three years previously, when my son was 14. This was a fearful and uncertain place for me to explore because I had a lot of guilt about the degree of hatred that I felt for my own son. But in the safety of the retreat and with the support of my partner, I was able to fully let go into my extreme anger.

I felt it with my whole body and raged with as much force as I could muster. I got in touch with a savage, primal place that wanted blood—and a lot of it. The more gruesome, the better. I wanted to kill my own son for what he had done to my daughter. I became the beast and let the anger consume me and express itself through me for about 15 or 20 minutes, until I was spent. The anger then gave way to tears coming from a place deep inside, as well as feelings of forgiveness.

That I had wanted to kill my own son was a hard truth to own. But it was my truth, and now that I have let it live, I can love my son even more. As Dale says, I can stop killing him in all the subtle ways I had been doing. I can now nurture and bless him in whatever he wants to be.
                                                                    —DAVID ANDERSEN*

Today we went and did Just Listening. I went into deep grief about our little unborn girl and how after five months when we found out I was carrying a boy after all, I had to bury the idea of having a daughter. I expressed my deepest, most inner thoughts and feelings and how I miss her in my life every single day. I shared the deep sense of loss I feel resenting, ignoring and carrying this huge coffin around with me all the time. We both said a little prayer for our little girl, the idea of my little girl who lived so alive in my heart and in my belly for five months. And then she died, and I had to bury that idea of her alone because Philip was elsewhere, otherwise engaged. I felt as if a part of me died when I buried her.

I said I still grieve her because lying right next to her in that coffin is my inner lost little girl. I grieve for all the lost pink in my life, all the choo-choos and the manicures never shared. I grieve the loss of being there watching her face fall in love for the first time, being there when she gets her first period, brushing her silky dark hair, and reading her Sleeping Beauty at night. I spoke of how Philip left me standing alone in the rain at her funeral. I shared all of it—including my inability to even look at a girl's clothing shop. All the hurt, all the pain that lives and breathes in me. Two little girls wrapped as one. My two losses.

Philip was totally with me and I know that he felt my pain very deeply. I was not asking him to fix it for me, just to know that our little girl had a name and that she was beautiful. And that I can see her little face smiling at me and sometimes I hear her whisper, "Wait, just wait." But maybe that's in my dreams alone. Our closeness was magnificent. Our intimacy was pure. And after all the resistance I had felt, my feelings now overflowed and I started to feel me in me.
                                                                    —DONNA BERBER

Work of sight is done.

Now do heartwork

On the pictures within you.

— RAINER MARIA RILKE

GUIDED HEARTWORK

Guided Heartwork (which you will find on track 5 of the Heartwork CD) gives you an opportunity to directly experience the "classical" Heartwork process of surrendering into and through layer after layer of your false self until you arrive back in your true home. You can do this exercise alone or with another person facilitating your process. In working with a facilitator, you may choose either to share your work or to work entirely internally, signaling the facilitator (with a pre-arranged signal) when you are ready to go on to the next step in the Heartwork process. Please refer to "Facilitator's Role" at the end of this section for suggestions about working with a facilitator.

The Heartwork process enables you to find your own unique way of looking into yourself. The following sequence, while representative of the stages that generally unfold during the course of a Heartwork session, may vary from person to person:

Getting Comfortable: In doing Heartwork, it is very important that you are physically comfortable. Being able to forget about your body as much as possible will allow you to focus all your attention on your internal process.

First, make any necessary adjustments in your environment. Where in the room would you be most comfortable? Where do you want your facilitator to be in relation to you, and in what bodily position? (It must be one that the facilitator is comfortable with.) If the room is too warm or too cool for your maximum comfort, adjust the temperature. If the room is too bright or dark, change the lighting. Adjust anything that interferes with your maximum physical comfort.

Now find the most comfortable position for your body. You may be most comfortable sitting erect, slouching, lying down (on your back, side or stomach) or in some other position. Ask your body what position it would most like to be in right now, and assume that position.

Settling In: Now close your eyes, take a few deep breaths, and allow yourself to relax as much as possible. If you have difficulty letting go of some of the surface tensions, just watch your breath come in and go out for a few minutes until you feel as relaxed as you can be at this time.

In the Heartwork you are about to do, it is very helpful to adopt an open, friendly, curious attitude towards whatever you encounter on your inward journey. This welcoming attitude will allow you to "witness" your process non-judgmentally, making it easier to see whatever is there because you have a more aware and less "attached" mind-state.

Defining the Problem: Now define your problem as clearly and concisely as possible. Or ask yourself, "What is it I would like to change as a result of doing this process?" If you enter into the Guided Heartwork process with no clearly defined issue, you can simply ask yourself, "Of all the issues that are present in my life, which one most needs my attention right now?" and allow the issue needing attention to choose itself by coming to the foreground. Another way to do this step is to ask, "If I had encountered a genie who was willing to grant me one wish, what would that wish be?" If some problem other than the one you had intended to work on demands your attention, even if it seems irrelevant to the original problem, trust it and go with that issue.

Locating the Problem: In the witness state of mind, now look around in your body to find the area where the problem is centered—experienced as blocked energy, stress, anxiety, tension or pain. ("Body" refers to that place where you experience not only physical sensations, but also senses in a more subtle way.) Notice how deep inside your body it sits. You can work with thoughts or mental metaphors, sensations, feelings or visual images in this process.

Clarifying: Keeping your attention focused in this inner feeling-space, describe in as much detail as possible what you experience here. If you have difficulty getting in touch with what is happening in this place, you may find it helpful to ask curious questions, such as: How big is it? What's its shape? What color is it? What is it made of? What is the texture of its surface? What does it smell like? What is the feel of this thing? What's it like? What would this part of me say if it could talk? Vivid visual imagery, memories and intense feelings often arise at this stage of the inward-looking process.

Focusing: Now slowly and carefully move your awareness toward and ultimately into the very center, or point of greatest intensity, of this feeling-space. You may find it helpful to follow these steps:

1. Start by allowing your awareness to get close enough to the feeling-space to be able to experience the energy coming out of it. (Kind of like feeling the heat a hot stove gives off when you walk past it.) What is emanating from this place inside you that you have spent most of your life avoiding?

2. Then make direct contact with the "surface" of the space. Can you get close enough to this thing inside yourself to actually "touch" the surface of it with your awareness? What is it like? How does it feel?

3. Then "move" into the surface layer. Can you find a way to get inside it, to become one with it, to experience what this surface layer that splits you in two is like from the inside? See if you can determine exactly what it is made of. Take your time so you can experience every step of this most incredible journey. In so doing, you will begin to see exactly how you work and who you really are—beyond all your ideas, beliefs and images of who or what you thought you were.

4. Then move through this layer into the interior while still being in contact with the surface (only now from the inside). What is it like to be inside it? How does it feel? What do you sense in this space? Rest here for a few minutes and let yourself be. Let whatever wants to come into your consciousness arise—thoughts, feelings, images, memories or sensations.

5. Allow yourself next to let go of your grip on the surface layer and let yourself be drawn inwards, downwards, towards the center or bottom or other end of this yearning space—much like a magnet would draw you toward something. Let yourself go—slowly and with great awareness, allowing whatever wants to be revealed to you to come into consciousness.

Penetrating: As you move inward, you may become aware of reluctance, resistance, hesitation or fear that prevents you from entering into the next space. Work with each barrier that you encounter, gradually softening into the resistance. Or you may find a different way to get through the barrier, such as plunging into it, embracing it, merging with it, being filled by it, looking directly at or into it, caring about or surrendering to it. Ultimately, it makes no difference what means you use; the moment you make the decision to face the barrier directly, the barrier begins to open by itself.

And by the way, don't assume extensive spiritual practice or years in therapy are prerequisites. Sometimes people who have never done a stitch of inner work in their lives come all the way home in one session. And sometimes those with the most experience have the most difficulty because they think they know what to do. As in all things, it is helpful to avoid expectations as much as possible.

Keep letting go, through layer after layer, until you get all the way to the center, bottom, end or other side of the inner space, or until you have gone as far as you feel you can go at this time.

Discovery: When you pass through this last barrier, you will usually enter into a wide-open space—experiencing a deep sense of peace, wholeness and oneness with the universe. Once you arrive here, or when you have gone as far as you can, rest in this space for a while. Remember what you went through to get here, so that you can find your way back whenever you want.

Look back at where you began this journey. Start with the problem you wished to change, as you originally defined it, and see how the work you have done relates to that problem. See how you created the suffering for yourself—how you moved out of this place of wholeness, connectedness and peace, how you forgot your deepest truth and how you became lost in fear, confusion and delusion. How can you relate differently to this problem when it arises in the future? Let yourself know that you can always return to this place whenever you are willing and that you can take however long it takes to come back again.

Re-entry: Now check to see if you wish to go further in the process of opening more deeply into the center of the problem. If you do, repeat any of the previous steps that would take you deeper, and continue the process until you are totally satisfied that you have gone as far as you can for now.

Closure: Do you feel complete? If not, take the time to say, feel or do whatever you need to in order to complete this experience. You may need to express feelings, integrate and assimilate insights or simply remain quiet.

FACILITATOR'S ROLE:

The most important aspect of the facilitator's role is the creation of a safe space in which the person doing the exercise may look inward. To best facilitate the work, it is important that facilitators:

- Maintain a nonjudgmental attitude. This means valuing equally every aspect of the other person's work and being and placing no expectations or demands on the person to do something that he or she is unwilling or disinclined to do.

- Clearly convey to the person doing the work that he or she is in complete control of the entire process from beginning to end, including setting the pace, determining the timing and direction the work takes, and deciding when the work has gone far enough for a particular time.

- Communicate caring by being totally attentive to what the person doing the work is experiencing in the moment. This means temporarily shelving the intellect, which analyzes, labels and compartmentalizes what it perceives. Occasionally, the facilitator may (with the person's permission or requesting) support, encourage and add energy to the other person's work by placing his or her hand(s) on the area(s) of the person's body where the attention is being focused.

- Be creative and keep the process moving. Engaging intuition, the facilitator balances probing with silence in moving with the other person toward the center of his or her experience. The degree to which the facilitator is in touch with the center of his or her own being is the degree to which the facilitator is able to guide the person to his or her center.

- Maintain an awareness that the thoughts, feelings and sensations that arise are not who we really are. Remaining fully attentive, but not attached to the content, the facilitator communicates to the other person that it is possible to look at and be with what is happening without being overwhelmed.

- Be willing to be "real" with the other person—that is, to acknowledge one's own humanity and refrain from creating an illusion of perfection. The facilitator needs to be willing to admit to, and openly deal with, the "mistakes" generated by his or her own shortcomings. When a facilitator pretends omniscience and sets himself or herself above the other person (even when the facilitator is a professional counselor and the other person is a client), the facilitator reinforces any sense of powerlessness and low self-esteem that the other person may already have.

- Sometimes it is helpful for the facilitator to share some of his or her own growth process. If, in the name of "professional distance," a counselor is unwilling to experience with a client the common humanity they share, both are robbed of the opportunity to share compassion (which means, literally, "to have passion with").

- Be aware that the facilitator is, at best, a catalyst for the other person's self-healing. In fact, one benefit of Heartwork is that it is reciprocal—providing both the facilitator and the person doing the exercise equal opportunity for looking inward.

*O*f the many sessions of Guided Heartwork I've done, one stands out above the rest for its intensity, clarity, and healing. It occurred during an eight-day retreat, an opportunity to really let go. I attribute the success of this experience to the group energy and the total commitment of my partner to my healing, which struck me at the time as being greater than my own commitment.

For the previous year or so, I had been bothered by chronic hip and pelvic pain, so that's what I decided to look into. As I lay on the floor and closed my eyes, I sank into the feeling and tried to visualize the pain in my pelvic region. Almost immediately, I saw in my mind's eye a vivid image of a medieval-looking, gray, metal, mace-type object, covered with spikes. It was elongated, more gourd-like or phallic-shaped. The first hit that I got was that it was not mine. I at once knew that it was the image my mother carried of me while I was in her womb, an image I had in a sense inherited it from her. This made perfect sense to me because years before, a deep knowing had come to me that the great sadness overriding every aspect of my mother's being was that she was a lesbian and had kept it hidden all her life. She never allowed herself to be who she truly was. As a result, she was the saddest person I have ever known. On some level I believe she hated men, in fact hated me, and did not want a male child growing inside her. This rejection might have been why I was born two months prematurely. Or perhaps I had sensed the rejection and did not want to be inside her and so caused my own early birth. In any case, this mace-like object was the image she carried during her pregnancy and that she then unintentionally transferred to me. I have carried it in my own way as a feeling of guilt for being male and also of shame about any expression of healthy male power and sexuality.

During the session, I next spoke directly to my mother, who was no longer alive, boldly saying, "Yes, I can be the most evil, destructive force imaginable. Don't fuck with me. But I am also a gentle, vulnerable and beautiful man."

A coughing fit then overcame me and I felt the image move up into my chest where I visualized it as a massive constriction made of concrete. I then remembered how a friend had recently told me what a sensitive and gentle person I was and that I must have gotten it from somewhere. The realization then came that this mass in my chest related to my father, and it was all the gentleness, vulnerability, and creativity that he never expressed through his entire lifetime. I grieved this and wept deeply both for him and for myself, and I forgave him.

I see what came to me during this session as "authentic" knowledge—information directly from the source and so deep that it is certain. I know these to be my truths, and they came from looking directly into my own being, with my body leading the way.

I was astonished at the speed at which this session developed. At times the flood of information was almost too much to keep track of. (Previous sessions of Guided Heartwork had progressed at a more gradual pace as I worked through layers to examine what was at the core.) As a result of this session, I was immediately freed of my pelvic pain, and it has not returned in the two years since.

—ALEX BRAND

I did a guided Heartwork session about losing my power and how that seemed to manifest in a large gray matter within myself. It was like a lump of cement that was connected to work and self-love. When I got in touch with it, I saw that the gray lump was my deadness, and that it is an integral part of me that comes and goes. I realized that my deadness is alive in me. It approaches me with tenderness, real tenderness, and it opens me up, rather than pushing me and shutting me down. If I don't ever feel dead, then how could I ever know what it feels like to be alive?

—DONNA BERBER

Where Have I Been?

Walking the garden
Slowly, consciously
Tasting the air,
Seeing the plants and trees,
Flowers and pathways,
Listening to music.
The babbling brook catches my eye.
I stop to listen to its music
And then sit on a rock,
Still, quiet, alone.
The constant flow and sound of the water,
The soothing distinctive sound.
It's here, each day, all day.
Yet this is a special and rare moment.
I just need to stop and notice,
Allow it all in,
And be soothed and filled.
Where have I been?

In the kitchen,
The evening meal.
The smells and the colors.
Peas and carrots offer vivid greens and oranges,
The vibrant simplicity of nature.
Rich, red, plump strawberries.
In that moment, their taste takes me back
To strawberry fields in a far away place
So distant that I had forgotten.
Bending, picking, packing, eating.
Where have I been?

The stars glisten tonight
Among the wispy clouds
In the magnificent night sky.
Stopping, looking, noticing,
I lean back, shouting aloud,
"Magnificent beauty!"
As if seeing it for the first time.
Where have I been?

The face of my bride
Twenty years later,
Soft skin, tender eyes, beautiful smile.
Reaching out for a gentle caress
As we did when we were dating.
Seeing, really seeing, each other.
A tingle in our touch.
How blessed we are to feel this way.
I think of the days
When I've looked and not seen,
Listened and not heard.
And now, as I absorb her beauty,
I wonder
Where have I been?

—PHILIP

AWARENESS MEDITATION

The Awareness Meditation (which you will find on track 6 of the Heartwork CD) teaches you to be present with your immediate experience in the moment—to open to the sensations, sounds, images, feelings and thoughts within your field of awareness in each moment—moment after moment after moment. This process strengthens your ability to face the difficult things you encounter on the journey inward; opens the mind to presence (pure awareness) and loosens the ego's attachment to thoughts, feelings and sensations by shifting one's identification from the ego to awareness. It dissolves the sense of a self that is separate from the world and creates a sense of inner spaciousness large enough to fully experience each and every experience as it happens, thereby ending the need to repress intense emotional events.

The Soft Body and Awareness Meditations are the two principal meditations that support the Heartwork process—in fact, they *are* the process. They are most effective when practiced together and, once mastered, can be practiced throughout the day. You can continually return to these two processes, checking in with yourself to see if you are present to sensations, sounds, images, feelings and thoughts and simultaneously letting go of any holding in the body. Practiced together faithfully, these two meditations will transform your life—guaranteed!

Awareness Meditation used to be difficult for me. Every time I did it, I'd think, "I can't do this. This is not working for me." I was sure my thoughts were too diffuse and frenetic or too vague and persistent for me to focus my mind on a part of my body. But what I have learned is that struggling against your thoughts doesn't do much. Letting them scatter and veer around is OK, as long as one thought (I imagine it as my breath sometimes or one part of my body, like my hands) has a single focus. Eventually then,

The worn shoes
rest on the doorway,
leather cracked and stained.
A thousand miles of wandering
has molded them to the shape
of your feet.

But now
you've stepped inside,
removed your socks,
and feel the yellow sunlight,
warm on the polished wood floor.

Wherever you walk now,
you are in your own body.

And whether on green grass
or sharp gravel,
Nothing stands now
between you and
the whole wide world.

— RICHARD WEHRMAN

it clicks and I'm present with myself. It may just last ten seconds or maybe even two minutes. There may even be some flare-ups of wayward thoughts here and there. But once I've experienced my body's calm and focus, any wayward thought seems less like a challenge and more like a passing train—you hear it, and its sound is almost calming. And then it's gone.

—CHIDSEY DICKSON

*I*n the Awareness Meditation, I reached the spaciousness. I felt like an astronaut floating in the vastness of space, able to do flips and freely float. Then Dale asked us to see our thoughts. I could see them, but I let them pass by. He then asked us to attach ourselves to thoughts, good and bad, to see and feel what happens. I noticed that whenever I did that, walls would come down around the thought to enclose it and I would go from this vast, boundless world to a constrained and bounded one. I noticed that the "walls" were my beliefs, prejudices, and feelings related to and attached to that thought. It happened with every thought I attached to—good or bad. When I attached to an anxious thought, I could feel my body tense up as if getting ready to defend itself. I could see how these barriers constrained me from seeing the truth as they tried to project their perception of the truth on me without allowing open assessment of what may or may not be different.*

After the exercise, we discussed our experience with our partners. I expressed my concern to Karen that absolutely every thought I attached to was bounded by these walls and that I was afraid that it wasn't something that we could change. Within a few minutes, Karen said something to me that would normally make me defensive. But I was open and didn't take her comments as personal affronts. Instead, I heard what she said as statements coming from someone who was trying to understand more so she could learn. In that moment, I realized that we can indeed separate from thoughts without creating these barriers made of our limiting beliefs. I realized that the reason these thoughts had the barriers was that they were each from a past state of unconscious reaction, but when I could operate in a fully conscious judgment-free mode, as I was then, there were no barriers. It was incredibly enlightening.

—BRIAN WILLIAM*

Have patience with everything unresolved in your heart and try to love the questions themselves *as if they were locked rooms or books written in a very foreign language.* Don't search for the answers which could not be given to you now, because you would not be able to live them. And the point is, to live everything. Live the questions now. Perhaps then, someday far in the future, you will gradually, without even noticing it, live your way into the answer.

—RAINER MARIA RILKE

INQUIRY

Inquiry is a dynamic, open-ended exploration into the immediacy of our experience to more deeply understand the mystery of who and what we truly are. The practice is based on a simple but profound principle: being freely reveals itself to anyone who loves to know the truth of reality and is willing to wholeheartedly surrender to not-knowing and remain open to and curious about truth. To paraphrase George Washington Carver's reply upon being asked how he discovered the thousands of uses for the lowly peanut, if you love something deeply enough, it will reveal all its secrets.

In Inquiry, one brings together all the qualities necessary for deep understanding and transformation developed through working with the previous tools:

- the gentleness, vulnerability, surrender, sensitivity and unconditional love developed in Unwinding and Soft Body Meditation
- the interest, curiosity, need to understand, commitment to truth, focus, strength, courage, willingness and deep intimacy developed in Guided Heartwork
- the steadfastness, witnessing, presence, openness, spaciousness, awareness and immediacy developed in the Awareness Meditation

The purpose of Inquiry is to see as deeply as possible into the truth of an issue. Inquiry requires—and develops—both a profound openness as well as a laser-like ability to focus your awareness. Without the openness, what you are inquiring into will not reveal itself. Unless it knows it's going to be received openly, it will remain unconscious, behind the wall you built to protect yourself from it. The intensity of your focused awareness needs to be equal to or greater than the intensity of the wall. These two qualities—openness and focus—must be accessed together if you are to see deeply into the source of the issue. It's as if you are patiently, persistently and determinedly boring into an issue with a laser beam of "What is this?" and receiving whatever is uncovered or revealed with the tender loving care you would have for your own child if he or she was experiencing what you are opening to—even though what you are opening to may not necessarily be gentle and loving.

You need to develop awareness so that you can stay present to the big picture (spacious, non-discriminating awareness) *and* simultaneously discriminate the parts (what you are inquiring into) from the whole—much like looking at something in the dark with both a searchlight and a spotlight operating together. If you lose the

It makes a sound like AHHHHHHHHHHHHH

It feels like silence and space

A place where I can hear again

Where the longing simply is

And the thread is like gravity itself

Drawing and pulling inward effortlessly

A tear and a smile

A tender calling

Into grace

Falling

Into the arms

Of the one

Who is always there

A silent cry explodes within my soul

As my knees bend into majestic mercy

For the LOVE that is always present

—DONNA BERBER

big picture of presence or pure awareness, you will not be able to inquire deeply into the heart of the matter because you will easily get caught in storytelling and re-telling (how many times do we fruitlessly replay our stories about ourselves and the way the world is?). While you need to be open as deeply as possible to your feelings in Inquiry, take care not to get caught in them, allowing them to turn the process into a deep emotional release. If deep feelings threaten to overwhelm the Inquiry process, in order to stay with the Inquiry, you will need to bring an awareness to the process that is greater than the intensity of the deep feelings. Likewise, take care not to go to the other extreme and suppress the deep feelings through philosophizing, psychologizing, projecting (putting onto others those parts of ourselves that we don't accept), attaching to the feelings that bring pleasure or rejecting those that bring discomfort. Try to see them as a detached observer would. This ability often takes time to master and comes with the development of powerful presence.

Yet the mind must ultimately be the servant to the heart. In Inquiry, you need to adopt an attitude of openness and curiosity. Curiosity is a heart quality that affects the mind—it comes out of our deepest yearning to know the truth. Inquiry usually feels like you are grappling with something—really needing to understand it. To support the curiosity, you may find it useful to keep a question running in the background of your consciousness: "What is this?" "What's that about?" "What's behind or underneath that?" "What does that mean?"—anything that will keep you looking increasingly deeper into the truth you are seeking. Ultimately, you want to be questioning every thought, feeling, sensation and image that comes into your consciousness, using each as a doorway to the next deeper layer of insight and understanding.

In Inquiry, there can be no manipulation, no agenda and no pre-conceived ideas about where the inquiry will lead. You need to get out of your own way and simply be with and surrender into whatever thoughts, feelings or images arise as they arise—just as they are. While you will usually have a starting point, this attitude of surrender and not-knowing allows the process to unfold in a natural, open-ended way. The truth is here and now and you can only see and experience it by looking more and more deeply into what is happening in the moment. By following the intelligence of the soul and surrendering to the deep yearning within, Inquiry takes you through layers and layers of conditioned self—the ego structures and defenses, the self-images and identities and the incessant mental activity of thinking and reacting—and leads you home to an experience of your essential qualities and ultimately a realization of your true nature.

You can do Inquiry with others or by yourself, so experiment to see which way works better for you. You can learn Inquiry only by experience—and lots of it. As you progress with this tool, you will find your own way with it.

The more you practice Inquiry, the more it will become your natural way of being in the world. So whenever you don't understand something or encounter a difficulty, instead of fighting it or running away from it, you will find yourself automatically asking, "What is this? What's happening here?" When the commitment to the truth becomes stronger than the commitment to protecting your self-image, you have become free in a most significant way. One of Japan's greatest Zen Masters, Dogen Zenji, said, "In the end, the final refuge is sustained practice." Sustained Inquiry has the power to transform your life.

Inquiry Questions: The question that is really eating at you is most likely the best question to begin with. If that or another burning question grabs you and doesn't let you go, go with it—let it take you wherever it takes you. In addition to asking yourself, "What is this?" or "What is this about?" the following questions may also be useful:

- Am I pushing, fighting or running away—or am I letting go into the truth of my being in the moment?
- What's in the way of my being completely present right now?
- What do I need right now? (Give yourself what you need, being careful to distinguish between need and want.)
- What do I *really* want? (Surrender into the wanting and yearning.)
- What am I experiencing right now? What am I feeling?
- What is real? What is the truth?
- What is happening here?
- In my present situation, what is being mirrored to me about myself?
- Who or what am I?
- Who do I think I am? Who am I taking myself to be?
- What am I pretending not to know?

(*Note:* While I have practiced my own brand of Inquiry since 1982, my understanding of the process has been deepened and broadened greatly by Alia Johnson, my Diamond Approach teacher, with whom I have been working since 2000. The Diamond Approach is a profound spiritual practice developed by A. H. Almaas that works through the psychological aspects to access the spiritual dimensions of being. Almaas' book, *Spacecruiser Inquiry* [Shambhala, 2002], gives a more detailed description of the process.)

It is more important, more thrilling, more satisfying and infinitely more valuable to know the Healer than to be healed. —ANONYMOUS

Not long ago, I had a boss who not only had no respect for me but was downright abusive. In our sessions, Dale often asks me why I stayed in my job. It seemed incredible that I would stay in such a violent situation that has so damaged my self-esteem. For quite some time, I felt trapped, hopeless and powerless to leave.

I started to slip into a mind-numbing depression and had trouble waking up to go to work. My whole body would be in pain, and I dreaded the thought of getting out of bed and getting ready for work. One morning, the dread shifted to terror. The terror turned to a deeper depression. As I lay in bed, part of me wanted to know what was happening and wanted it to turn around. It wanted to know why I had created this painful and frightening relationship. I started to gently inquire into what was behind the depression, and I asked myself why I felt so helpless and hopeless.

I took a deep breath, and a memory came flooding back from when I was four years old. My mother used to wake me at 5:00 each morning and drop me off at a babysitter's place, where I would stay until it was time to go to school. All of the children in her care were verbally and physically abused. She was very rigid with us and any small diversion from what she wanted was punishable with a public spanking—without clothing. I was paralyzed in terror the whole time I was there. This memory was so real to me that I actually felt as though I was really back there again. I became nauseous and the terror of being small and frightened and helpless overwhelmed me.

I told my mother the babysitter was hurting me, and I begged her not to take me there. But she didn't hear me, and after awhile, I gave up asking for help. I shut down and suppressed my needs and feelings. I became a depressed child, subjected to the babysitter for years—until she was shut down for abusing children!

After this Inquiry experience, I cried for that little girl who needed help and could not get it. I had tremendous compassion for her and decided that I could not expect someone who had been abused in that way to be functioning effectively. The next time my boss was abusive, I gave notice.

—MADELINE STEWART

I was feeling a little stuck and so I started to look at that, and I came across my solar plexus and the buzz that lives there, that is always on. I let myself feel the charge that went through my whole body. After awhile, the hole in my center closed up and I went deep, deep into bliss. I also encountered my snake, and I realized he is part of what keeps me awake at night—constantly, vigilantly guarding me. He's a kind old snake, as old as I can remember. We have started a dialogue, and we agreed that he can start to just ease up a little. He is tired. He's been working so very, very hard for so long, guarding my (inner) little girl. He has known that I haven't been ready before.

Later, I discovered more about the purpose of my snake. He's a guardian of my grief. When I asked him what he needed, he said, "Play with me." I asked, "How do I play with you?" He answered, "Enjoy yourself more; have fun in what you do; be present when you're doing it; lighten up; don't take yourself so seriously. You can do it all, have it all and be it all."

I know I have work to do with my snake. I know that I need to befriend him and stop being afraid of him. He wants to play. I feel that this process will take me a little further each time I allow it.

— DONNA BERBER

I'm looking into the anxiety that permeates my daily experience. It lives throughout my entire body but seems to be centered in my belly. In making contact with it, I immediately become aware that I use anxiety to mute my fear and make it more manageable. I approach this fear in my belly gently, and when I make contact with a layer of sadness directly underneath the fear, the fear disappears. What am I sad about? I have to be very gentle with this inquiry, because I know that whatever is in there is frightened, vulnerable and not willing to expose itself.

My breathing begins to relax and the tension in my belly starts to release. My body stretches and then sits up straight. I become more alert. Warmth fills me. Then I begin to experience nausea, and the sadness becomes stronger. I rock back and forth, as if to soothe the sadness. It feels like grief. I sit gently with the grief, wondering what it is about. In touch with the grief, I notice that all the anxiety is gone. This feels like the deeper truth. I sigh and yawn. It is 4:30 in the morning. I feel deep exhaustion from decades of pushing myself to avoid dealing with this grief. What is it?

I focus more intently into my body where the grief is centered. I get very still with it, and I am aware of how everything begins to settle down. I sit patiently in the silence, and it feels like the silence is nourishing my entire being. The image of a woman-friend *who is the manifestation of Mother Earth's love comes to mind, and I am touched by her deeply healing warmth. I am more aware of my breath and the nourishment it brings.*

I am feeling very peaceful now, and it occurs to me that what I am grieving is the loss of this peace that is my natural state. Why would I repeatedly leave this state when it feels so very good, so right? I sit with this question for a long time and nothing comes except my teacher's voice saying, "I never answer why questions!" I pick up the inquiry again later on. I become aware that what keeps the anxiety running is the fear that I won't do something that needs to be done and that something terrible will happen as a result. So I'm always pushing myself to make sure everything gets done. And of course, that's impossible.

So I'm never at peace, except when I'm doing some kind of inner work like this that brings me into presence. This realization saddens me even more. It seems like a hopeless situation, much like being on a hamster wheel that's endlessly turning. Again, I realize that when I'm present, I'm not feeling driven. It's only when I'm not present—when the unconscious is running the show—that I feel so anxious. So all I need to do is remember to get present. I make a commitment to take time throughout the day to get present—at least a minute or two every hour. That feels like a good start.

Later still, I realize that although this resolution will make a big difference, it doesn't get at the root of the issue. So I pick up the thread again and ask myself why am I so afraid I will forget to do something vital, and what am I afraid will happen if I do? All I can get is this sense of impending doom, that something awful will happen.

Then I recall being 16 years old, riding in the car with my father, when he turned to me and told me I was a disappointment to him. I was shocked, devastated. My father meant a great deal to me, and for him to tell me that was the worst thing that he could have said. I also remember taking an oral final exam in school and could not answer the question. I remember feeling so humiliated. I was a good student and thought of myself as the smartest student in the class. The experience severely damaged my sense of who I was. I realize that I now live in continual fear of ever feeling these kinds of wounds again.

I see that I am trying at all costs (even running myself into the ground) to protect the image I have created of myself as a committed, competent, reliable person with great integrity. That's what my anxiety is all about. So I guess the real question for me is, "What do I really want—to be inflated with a false sense of self, or to be simple and real?"

—LAWRENCE ABRAHAM*

FREEZE FRAME

Freeze Frame allows you to use the material of your daily life to access the deeper issues that keep you from having what you really, really want. Try to set aside some time every day (ideally in the evening) to review events and see where you created some level of dis-ease in your being. It is usually best to begin with the issue that you had the most intense reaction to. Often the biggest issue relates to your loved one, and so the technique for working with a partner is included separately below. Here are the steps:

1. Review the incident needing understanding in as much detail as possible, as if you were watching a video in slow motion, paying particularly close attention to what you were thinking and feeling, especially immediately before the moment you felt the upset.

2. Replay in your mind the few moments immediately before the upset, this time in very slow motion, paying even closer attention to what you were feeling.

3. When you get to the exact moment where the upset happened, freeze the frame at precisely that point. Keeping your awareness focused directly on this moment, allow yourself to be totally open and vulnerable (what I call "taking the hit") and see what that touches in your consciousness.

4. At this point, you may use any of the previously learned tools that feel appropriate to take you as deeply as possible into the source of your discomfort.

For use in relationship: In any conflict, both individuals are 100 percent responsible for the creation of the problem. Freeze Frame creates the possibility for two (or more) people to look together—from the same side—at an incident that caused a painful rift in the relationship. Both can then take full responsibility for creating the problem and each can see how and why he or she created the issue to begin with. This ends the blaming and the "who's right, who's wrong" dance. For Freeze Frame to be effective, both parties need to be committed to discovering the truth in themselves, as opposed to defending a position.

1. Partner A relates the incident needing healing to Partner B in as much detail as possible, paying particularly close attention to what A was thinking and feeling, especially immediately before the moment A felt hurt by B.

2. Partner A replays the few moments immediately before the hurt, this time in very slow motion, paying even closer attention to what A was feeling.

3. When Partner A gets to the exact moment where the hurt happened, A freezes the frame at precisely the point where the blow was dealt. A does not move A's awareness away from this moment in time, but instead drops his or her defenses, stays totally open, takes the hit, and sees what it touches in A's consciousness.

4. That pain, if allowed, will eventually take Partner A back to an earlier (usually much earlier) pain that needs healing. A will see how he or she co-created the pain so that A can open the door to heal the old wound. (Have you ever noticed how we recreate the same pain over and over in our lives until we finally stop running away from the pain and see what it's trying to tell us?)

5. Once partner A has seen into the source of his or her pain, he or she can look at Partner B in precisely the same "freeze the frame" moment and see and feel where B was coming from. In this place of open awareness, the heart contains only compassion, understanding and forgiveness.

6. Partners A and B reverse roles and repeat the process.

(*Please note:* For more relationship tools, see the "Do It Yourself" section of the Heartwork Institute website, www.awakentheheart.org.)

....

*U*sing Freeze Frame has helped me look closely at how I anticipate the future and hold resentments about the past and it allows me to let them go. I had been causing myself tremendous pain by holding onto the emotions long after the actual, physical pain was gone.

Reliving a moment of physical abuse, I was able to freeze the moment just before being slapped in the face. The reality of that moment was that there was no pain. My mind was programmed to anticipate what was coming, which manifested as fear. I could see the anger in the eyes and facial expression of the one about to hit me. Advancing one frame later, the hand came closer, and my fear then turned to anger—mirroring the image before me. I advanced the frame again. Flesh hit flesh. In that moment, there was physical pain, but it paled in the light of the emotional pain. My mind went wild; fear and anger combined and I turned it inward. Afraid to strike back, I felt small, inferior, *and I blamed myself for being in this position. This pattern has stayed with me for years; each time a man raises his voice to me or curses in front of me, I anticipate physical abuse and am bathed in fear.*

Taking away both the anticipation and the aftermath, I was able to stay present with what was really happening. As I stayed with the frozen frame of flesh touching flesh, I was able to get to the point of no pain. Suddenly I could feel my body relaxing, tension leaving my shoulders, the tightness around my mouth and my throat lessening. All that was really there was flesh touching flesh—everything else was just my mind spinning its own story.

—MARCIE GASS

*M*y boss was talking about his newborn baby, and I was really enjoying hearing *about her. I mentioned that my mother was coming to drop off a gift for her, and quite suddenly he quite harshly stated that he was not allowing anyone near his baby for two weeks and that I was to tell my mother not to come. I felt very hurt and even ashamed at being scolded.*

Then I started to feel angry and was getting an attitude. Recognizing that this was my usual response to these types of situations, I made a conscious decision that I did not want to continue to feel hurt every time I felt confronted unexpectedly. So I turned to Freeze Frame.

I started with my initial feeling, which was intense shame and embarrassment at being scolded publicly. That led me to remember my mother saying quite often that, "we are not the beautiful people, therefore we do not belong and do not get to go to all the places that beautiful people can go." I felt really angry about that, and I put my anger onto my boss, saying to him in my mind, "Who do you think you are? Do you think you are better than us? Do you think my family is going to pollute your home and defile your precious little baby?"

I realized that this was not the root issue because I was still placing anger and blame outside myself. So I tried to zero in on the precise moment my reaction began. I sat with it for a little while and was able to discern that my initial reaction was intense pain and heartache—deep loss and longing. I had become a little baby myself in that moment that my boss came at me so fiercely. I felt the pain of not being protected when I was so vulnerable in the way he was protecting his newborn. I realized I was feeling the loss of not having that fierce protection from those I needed it from the most. Furthermore,

I was able to see that I had not developed the Protector in myself, and in that moment I had abandoned my "little baby" the way I was abandoned when I was little.

The experience taught me that I have grieving to do about the pain I feel from not being thought of as precious and worth "defending to the death." I learned that I recreate this pain a great deal in my life. I learned that I need to be my own protector and to know that I am worth defending and that I do not deserve to be treated harshly by others or by myself.

*—GRACIE TAYLOR**

When I attended my first Heartwork retreat, I had been seeing a counselor for several years to help me with the pain of loving and at the same time hating and fearing a family member. I had always considered him to be special, but almost each time we were together, he would make some critical comment about me or tell an out-and-out lie (usually in front of other people) that would hit me like a Mack truck.

I was fearful to be around him because I was always waiting for the next hit. Bottling up my emotions, I walked on eggshells. I had not been successful in letting go of the effect he was having on me, so I saw no other way but to learn how to let go of the relationship itself. That was my goal for the retreat.

When Dale taught us Freeze Frame, I found it painful to visualize and relive these scenes with my family member, but I focused on him and froze the frame just before he delivered "the hit." But what happened next surprised me. When I looked at his face and into his eyes, what I saw was an unhappy person—a person in pain. I could see that he was so unhappy and broken inside. I felt so sad for him, and I realized that it was his pain and unhappiness that was causing him to do and say all those horrible things. None of his actions had anything to do with me. For the first time, I was able to see him from a loving place. I was able to understand and forgive him. It is still hard for me to take the hits, but I no longer need to let go of the relationship. I learned to let go of how I felt instead. When a situation with him arises, I can Freeze Frame his eyes in my mind, and I am free.

*—NATALIE STECK**

Awake
In the 5 a.m. dark before dawn
I burrow deeper under the covers
I don't fall asleep
I'm awake.
I lie there

Winter Morning

Curled in a warm pocket.
When I rise
The house still sleeps.
I treasure the early morning
Silence now is mine.
I set up the coffee pot,
Grind the beans,
Inhale the distillation,
Start the coffeemaker.
The dog stands by the door
Impatient for release.
I unlock the front door,
Admit the frozen morning,
She charges out—an eighty-pound shepherd
I refuse to walk—
Too much power to restrain
When she lunges out the door.
Moments later
Before the coffee is brewed
Insistent barks break the silence.
Consider the sleepers.
Gird myself to confront the cold:
Wool socks, red fleece-lined black jeans,
Sweater over turtleneck,
Pull on hat, lined gloves,
Insulated winter boots,
Down-filled parka.
Ready.
From the top of the wooded slope
So still I hear the soft crashing
Of ice floes in the river below.
Tree shadows darken the snow
Luminescent in the moonlight.
Dog motion in the trees,
I summon her, "Jesse,"—
In Hebrew "God exists."
But intent she pays me no mind,
Pretends not to hear her name.
I whistle, the whistle I practiced as a child,
To call other loved dogs.
She only wanders further into the woods
Terrorizing the darkness that delights her.

—FRANCES RAPPORT

HEARTWORK IN ONE'S DAILY LIFE

What follows are brief descriptions of some auxiliary exercises that many people find helpful on their inner journey. The first exercise is useful in learning how to stay in the moment. The others help to bridge the gap between more exclusively inner work and "outer work," or being in the world.

Continuum of Awareness: This is a technique taught in the Diamond Approach wherein you simply verbally report to a partner whatever you are experiencing moment-to-moment—sensations, sounds, images, thoughts, feelings, energies, etc. There is no particular focus, just an intention to feel your own subtlety and innerness. The attitude is one of delicacy. The partner tries to be there with deep attention, following the other's process in a simple, delicate way.

Sleep Meditation: In addition to the Soft Body and Awareness Meditations, this exercise is very useful to help fall asleep or fall back to sleep. Simply get in the most comfortable position you can find, and then don't move a muscle. The reason this works is that most of the time, we can't sleep because your mind is overactive. By paying attention to your thoughts, you feed the thinking process and keep it going, thereby assuring your sleeplessness. But by focusing your attention on your body (which you must do in order not to move a muscle), you starve the thinking process, and the thoughts slow down and eventually die altogether. In addition, by paying attention to your tired body, your body will naturally let go into sleep.

Walking Meditations: Books have been written on the intricacies of walking meditation, but for the purposes of this book, I will keep the instructions very simple. In Heartwork retreats, I teach the following three walking meditations:

Soft Body Walking Meditation: Walk attentively in a circle or back and forth, taking steps only when the body is completely "soft" or open (see Soft Body Meditation for more details).

Awareness Walking Meditation: Walk attentively in a circle or back and forth, taking steps only when you are totally present (sensing, looking and listening).

Soft Body–Awareness Walking Meditation: Walk attentively in a circle or back and forth, taking steps only when the body is completely soft and you are totally present.

Conscious Eating: Be attentive to the entire process of eating your food—from the creation of the meal all the way through the digestive process. We rarely even taste our food, let alone notice things like when our appetite is satiated or when we are physiologically (as opposed to emotionally) hungry. In this exercise, the point is to be totally aware and conscious of how the food tastes, what temperature it is, what the texture is like, the sound of your fork scraping on the plate, etc. Living in awareness includes all of our activities—walking, eating, breathing, and so forth.

Do Nothing Meditation: This is the simplest but most difficult of all meditations. Doing nothing means doing nothing. You cannot try to do nothing, because trying is doing something. This is a meditation you need to simply leap into. And leaping into it takes you beyond your ordinary self into a state of presence.

Other activities that increase your ability to be present and also coax essential aspects of your being to come forth include listening to music, dancing, communing with nature, speaking with awareness and, ultimately, doing your work in the world with awareness.

Half Light

In the morning darkness
I pull on yesterday's wrinkled
pants and shirt and feel in the dim light
for my glasses and sandals.

Shuffling downstairs I set
the thermostat against the morning chill
and feed the cats on
little paper plates.

As the coffee gurgles
into the pot
I stare out the window over
the kitchen sink.

Squinting,
trees and bushes bloom
from the dark grey violet
blanketing the yard.

A squirrel shivers and
shakes his tail;
a jay swoops and lands
 upon the feeder.

In the half light
I stare at my transparent
reflection in the window—
half myself and half
the blue world outside.

Bit by bit the dim world brightens,
until I dissolve completely,
and only the new day
remains.

—RICHARD WEHRMAN

The Human heart has the extraordinary capacity to hold and transform the sorrows of life into a great stream of compassion.

—BUDDHA

THE JOURNEY CONTINUES

I live my life in widening circles

that reach out across the world.

I may not complete the last one

but I give myself to it.

—RAINER MARIA RILKE

Some people come to this work with a specific issue that they need to resolve. This may be a personal crisis, an illness or a difficult life situation. While one or two Heartwork sessions or events are often sufficient for resolution of a particular issue, this work may bring up deeper, more fundamental issues that one may choose to explore in future Heartwork experiences.

Others are drawn to Heartwork because they feel something is lacking in their lives or because they feel compelled by an inner urge for greater depth and wholeness. These people choose to participate in Heartwork sessions and events on a more regular basis so that they can discover, come to trust and incorporate into their daily lives their own inner-working process. With experience, people develop the ability to be deeply present with themselves and their lives.

The Heartwork process eventually becomes self-sustaining. When we acknowledge our pain and look into its source, we release energy—and we discover that our freedom lies in the very center of our pain. The resulting understanding generates a willingness to face the circumstances of our lives, while the resulting openness strengthens our resolve to live fully in each moment.

Each opening that occurs then becomes not the end of the process, but rather a new beginning.

PART III: HEARTWORK STORIES

Through the gateway of feeling your weakness
Lies your strength.

Through the gateway of feeling your pain
Lies your pleasure and joy.

Through the gateway of feeling your fear
Lies your security and safety.

Through the gateway of feeling your loneliness
Lies your capacity to have
Fulfillment, love and companionship.

Through the gateway of feeling your hopelessness
Lies true and justified hope.

Through the gateway of accepting the lacks in your
Childhood lies your fulfillment now.

—EVA PIERRAKOS
Pathwork Lecture 190

For the raindrop,
joy is entering the river—
Unbearable pain becomes its own cure.

—MIRZA GHALIB

(as translated by Jane Hirshfield)

BRIEF THERAPY ENCOUNTERS

Private therapy sessions offer individual guidance and teaching for either working through a specific issue or for doing the inner work that Heartwork offers. These sessions generally occur in my office or over the telephone and last anywhere from 45 minutes to four hours. Most people I work with choose to have regular bi-weekly, weekly or semi-weekly sessions, while others come on an as-needed basis. Most are able to work through the issues they bring to resolve in a few months. Occasionally, people require only one or two sessions for their issues to be worked through completely. Some will totally resolve an issue and then return months or years later to work on another issue. Some have such profound experiences with Heartwork that they see it as a way of living; these people choose to do ongoing work with me until they feel they no longer need my guidance.

The following accounts of Heartwork experiences were written by people with whom I have worked over the past 25 years. The descriptions are representative of the way Heartwork unfolds. Those names in this chapter followed by an asterisk (*) are pseudonyms.

GAIL*

I made an appointment with Dale Goldstein on the recommendation of a doctor I had seen for stress and anxiety. For twelve years, I had been treated for a hyperactive intestine, a nervous stomach and nerves—sometimes with a fair degree of success, but lately, with no success. The medications prescribed for me covered a wide range: Mylanta, Librax, Pathibamate, Combid Spansules, Ludiomil, Tagamet and Valium. When one ceased to work, my doctor would prescribe another. Eventually, nothing seemed to work. I was constantly plagued by a series of physical symptoms, and three years prior my doctor recommended that I see a psychiatrist. I did this weekly for approximately seven months. During that time, the long periods of depression and crying that I had experienced began to fade (with the help of Valium), but I never felt totally comfortable or in control of my life. Without warning, the symptoms would recur. My stomach always seemed to be affected by my nervousness, and as a result, my professional, sexual and social lives were affected. The physical symptoms also varied, and they seemed to become centered in an aching, constricted feeling in my throat and a tension in my tongue, which made it impossible to relax.

At my appointment with Dale, I first gave him this medical background, and we spent the better part of an hour getting to know each other. I emphasize "each other" because it was so different in this respect from my experience with the psychiatrist. In that situation, he knew everything about me, but I was not allowed to know the smallest detail about him. It was hard to remember that I was dealing with a human being. I was never comfortable with the arrangement, so after very little good was accomplished, I terminated the sessions.

Dale gave me a brief autobiography, including why he was doing this work and how he had gotten into it. He explained the ideas behind Heartwork. I understood from his explanation that the procedure involved talking as in psychiatric consultations, but that the verbal therapy was coupled with the touching of arms, head and stomach. I must admit that I was leery about the success of the treatment, but I felt that Dale was a strong, trustworthy person who obviously believed in what he did because he had seen it work. That, plus the fact that I was at my wits' end from the symptoms I was suffering, made me game for anything that sounded remotely reasonable.

Dale then explained the basic steps of this therapy: 1) State your goals or what you want to accomplish in the briefest, clearest way possible; 2) Get relaxed; 3) Focus your attention on the physical symptoms that are the result of the anxiety or problem; 4) Look deeply into the problem through feelings or images that might arise, and thereby, 5) See into the source of the problem.

Dale told me that everyone progresses through these stages at different rates, and that some find it impossible to get beyond recognizing the problem. I felt ready, even anxious, to begin. Dale also told me that he gets gut feelings from people, and that he felt that I was ready to face what had been disturbing my life for thirteen years.

My goal: I felt that I was an affectionate person, but I had trouble expressing my feelings to two people whom I love very much—my older daughter (age 7) and my husband. I wanted to be able to unselfconsciously kiss and hug my daughter and to make love to my husband without the feelings of guilt and sadness that usually accompanied and interfered with the act. Also, I felt that I let other people influence me in my decisions, and I wanted to be free from their effect.

I climbed onto the massage table in Dale's office and lay on my back with something under my knees to raise them. Dale closed the blinds so that the room was in semi-darkness. He sat on a stool next to me near my head. I felt very much at ease. Dale asked me to pinpoint the area in my body where I felt the most stress. It was my tongue. He directed me to try to focus my attention under my tongue. An image came quickly, and even though it seemed ridiculous, I told him it was a light bulb. I spent a few minutes examining the light bulb and describing it in response to Dale's questions. What did it look like? Pear-shaped. What color? Filmy, yellowish. Was it attached to anything? No. Was it on? Yes. Use its heat to warm and relax your tongue. Is it working? Yes.

Dale told me that I could call on this image again and again to help me relax. Through all of this, Dale intermittently placed his arm next to mine or on my throat or head, but it wasn't an obtrusive presence. It simply felt like someone who cared was there with me.

Next, Dale asked me where the second area of stress in my body seemed to be. The answer was easy; my throat was constricted and tense. This and the tension I felt in my tongue had made talking and swallowing difficult and eating at times impossible. Dale asked me to describe the feeling, and I immediately received a visual image. I asked if he meant for me to describe an image. He said not necessarily, but I knew I had to, and I began by telling him that I had known this would happen. There was a part of my background that I hadn't told him before, but I also had decided that I would tell him eventually, when it became important for me to do so. I told him now: I had had an abortion thirteen years before. I was unmarried; my current husband was the father. I agreed that an abortion was the only answer for three reasons. First, I was terrified to tell my father. Second, I had just graduated from college (the first of five children to do so) and had gotten my first real job. Third, my boyfriend's family would have seen the unplanned pregnancy as a failure after he had tried so hard to prove that he was independent.

The image in my throat was a baby, and I gave Dale the details in piecemeal fashion with long pauses in between. I was crying, but I didn't care. He asked me what the baby was doing. It took time to focus on the image and decide, but I thought he was sleeping. I repeatedly referred to the baby as "he." Dale directed me to wake the baby, pick him up and get to know him. In my mind, I did so, but when he asked me to try to become one with the baby, I sensed a great deal of interference. Dale asked me what was in the way, and I answered that I was afraid the baby hated me. I was sobbing uncontrollably by that point. Dale suggested that I look right into the baby's eyes and try to become the baby. When I did this, I heard a conversation that went something like this:

Me:	*Do you know who I am?*
Baby:	*Yes.*
Me:	*Are you happy? [The baby was smiling at me.]*
Baby:	*Yes.*
Me:	*What do you need to know from me?*
Baby:	*Why?*
Me:	*Why did I have the abortion?*
Baby:	*Yes. Why?*

That one word was the final brick holding the dam. The dam burst, and I explained why. Then I had one final question for the baby.

"Do you hate me?" I asked.
Smiling, SHE answered, "No."

The baby was a girl. Her face was my daughter's face. I can see it again now through the tears in my eyes. I told Dale the baby wasn't a boy, but a girl. He said, "Yes, I know. She's your daughter, she's you." This was a significant enough disclosure, but when I realized that Dale was crying, too, I was truly touched.

I lay there rethinking the whole experience. It was now apparent to me that I had harbored hostile feelings toward my father, who had since died, because I had never felt that I could tell him I was pregnant. This now seemed insignificant. The problem was with my husband and his part in my decision to have an abortion. I realized that it was really not his fault, but mine. I had just never been strong enough to object and to do what I knew to be right. I let him make my decision, and then I felt angry with myself for letting him do so.

I could also now admit that I had taken all the guilt I felt as a result of having the abortion, murdering a baby as I saw it, and misplaced it every time I looked at my daughter. I was afraid of her judgment of me if she knew what I had done. Now, I knew I could change all of that and make it up to her. I truly felt that I had paid my dues.

I relaxed for a few minutes. I then got up from the table, and Dale said he wanted to show me something. He led me to a mirror where I confidently met my own stare. My eyes were different.

I felt exhausted, euphoric and a bit embarrassed. It was as though a stranger and I had shared an experience not unlike delivering a baby.

Since that day, the physical symptoms I had known for thirteen years have not recurred. I have felt confident in my decisions and affections. I backslide a little at times, but I can get back, by myself, to the point where Dale brought me. This is the closest I ever expect to come to a miracle.

MARCIE

I'd been trying to work with why I have had such a difficult time accepting gifts and had tried several approaches on my own. First, I acknowledged that the problem existed. That was not difficult because whenever someone tried to give me a gift, I felt anger rising. Then I could feel my throat constrict, my back become painfully tight between the shoulder blades, and my arms tense. I wanted to flail and hit the giver of the gift. I wanted to scream, "How could you do this? Why are you hurting me?" Then, I tried observing what was happening and how I was feeling. I did not try to understand it or see where it was coming from, but instead I just tried to observe it, softening into the feelings. But after months of trying this, I wasn't getting anywhere but frustrated. So next, I practiced more concentrated breathing, not resisting anything. This quieted the feelings of anger but still left my body tense. The restlessness proved helpful because it allowed me to admit I was stuck and needed help.

I made an appointment with Dale to let him know that I was stuck and asked his support in not letting me out of the conversation when I got to his office. This proved to be a good strategy because I surely wanted to change the focus once we were face-to-face. With Dale's guidance, and feeling supported by his presence, I was able to quickly get in touch with what was happening inside my body and mind. The anger was quiet, but it was there, and the longer I stayed with it the more compassionate and protective I felt towards it. However, that inner space was being shared with another fierce anger that seemed to come from behind me. I knew I needed to face this, too, and Dale encouraged me to do so. That is when I learned the lesson of backing up. When turning to face my fear seemed too difficult a task, I let myself back slowly into it. The closer I got, the quieter it became, until I was finally able to lean into it and rest there. The fear also seemed to rest and even to soften. It, too, was feeling wounded and wanted to be held and comforted.

Feeling at peace and supported, I then focused on the idea of accepting gifts. Closing my eyes, I pictured three of those gifts spread out before me and, breathing gently, I then watched a barricade form between me and the gifts. I could feel the physical tensions rising once more, although the old anger was gone. Slowly, the barrier moved toward me and more pain began to grip my torso. As I watched, freezing each frame of action as the barrier continued to move toward me, the scene shifted. The barrier became arms that held me in a vice grip.

That is when I thought it all became clear. I was sure they were the arms of my father, who had taken me, as his "gift," many times. It wasn't until a short time later that the words I'd chosen, "vice grip," struck me like a sledgehammer. Vice grips were in my grandfather's workshop. What I had been trying to forget all these years was that he had raped me, too, in this place. I have spent a lifetime trying to brush the sawdust-filled memory of that experience from my body. Because I felt that I was a gift that had been taken, I would spend the rest of my life in fear of receiving—especially from men.

Now, I am beginning to see that these two men were also gifts to me. Gifts I didn't want, but nonetheless gifts that helped shape how I defined myself in the past. As I receive the notion that they were gifts, I am able to start redefining who I am now.

Because of the work I have done and am doing in Heartwork, I feel totally calm, in my head, as I let the tension of the inner pain do what it has to do. Heartwork has taught me to be patient and still and not to resist when pain occurs. How freeing it is to be an observer of pain and not to be swallowed up by it—not to believe that I AM the pain. I am content—no, overjoyed!—to know that by making Heartwork a lifestyle, my journey through this life is now something I can embrace as I look forward to the next unfolding.

KEN

My individual session began about 2:00 pm on a Friday afternoon, allowing Dale and me about four to five hours to work. I knew we would have plenty of time and that I could really relax into the experience—truly let down and stretch out.

For the first hour or so, we spoke casually face-to-face about several recent themes in my inner work, including my ability to access fear and vulnerability. We then shifted gears for some experiential inner work, and I lay down on my back with my head on a pillow as Dale sat by my side. I closed my eyes and began to pay more attention to my breathing, the general feeling of my body and the volume of my voice, which gradually quieted and seemed to come from a more personal, private, gentle place inside of me.

My speech slowed as it became attuned to my breath and to the subtle sensations and emotions that were beginning to surface.

I felt some heaviness, a sense of darkness, but nothing threatening—maybe duskiness is a better word. It was a feeling of weight, vulnerability and burden. Dale asked me where it was in my body and what shape it took. I outlined the shape on my chest and described its three-dimensional form. Dale asked me what surrounded the shape, and I was surprised to sense a light, feathery aura-like energy around it. This surprised me, because I had been anticipating a clearer, sharper boundary.

The sensations in my chest became more vivid and my feelings more pronounced as we talked about my family and our home life when I was a child. It felt as though I needed to create more time and space for the feelings by reducing the words we were exchanging. We were talking about the heaviness and the feeling of being burdened and relating it to growing up with my family when I uttered the phrase, "It was all too much." This phrase seemed to connect me most directly to my fear and sadness about feeling overwhelmed by my family and the characteristic ways my family members interacted. I continued to repeat the phrase, and as I did so, I felt a sensation of streaming energy rush from my throat down to my abdomen. I continued to say the phrase, elaborating upon it some, and then I began to cry. The sadness, vulnerability and helplessness that I felt in my family as a young boy began to register in my mind and body. I cried gently for a few minutes with my chest periodically heaving and quivering involuntarily. Gradually, my crying subsided. I continued to feel sad, but I also felt quiet and peaceful and open. These feelings had existed within me for so many years, and I'd wanted to express them for so long. This fertile experience has proved a tremendous breakthrough for me, leaving me with a great sense of hope.

ELIZABETH[*]

*H*ow long does it take to make sense out of a broken past? How many years will it take to heal wounds set deep and unreachable by the injury of growing up in a violent, alcoholic home?

I've been actively trying to sort out the mess of my pain for many years. The tools I used—alcohol, drugs and denial—were not always the best. Only when I was able to separate myself from the urge to move away from the pain did I begin to heal. I began to see the truth that lay under all the hurt: my dad was not well. This revelation is new and has split me to the core.

The awareness about my dad began to unfold the day I let the thought into my consciousness that I was not well. Having spent seven years in sobriety, I was surprised to realize that I had not fully accepted this fact. It took sustained bodily pain from a back injury to open me to this awareness. After three years of coping with constant pain, I admitted to myself that I had lost a part of my health and finally began to grieve that loss.

Feeling small and undefended, I let myself express the feelings that move in me like a tide seeking its level every day. Feelings I had not allowed anyone, not even myself, to see came rushing out. I spoke of the pain I experience each day, how I could not master or solve it, how vulnerable I felt and how much a part of me absolutely hated being in that state.

And the next thing that broke open in my consciousness was that my father was not well. It hit like a tidal wave. After decades of railing against the anguish he caused, I suddenly felt as though his pain was a part of me—as though it were my own. The agony of losing him to alcoholism wrenches me. And I see, I finally see, that he was not well.

That's all.

He was not well.

I find myself torn apart over and over by this realization. Care-worn images of the torment rained down on me as a result of his disease—memories I've cradled close—pale in comparison to this understanding. The memories no longer feel like a lifeline keeping my anger alive. This puzzles a part of me not ready to let go of the hurt and resentment. I cry for the loss of his health and for my own loss of him as though they are inseparable—and I realize they are inseparable.

Something in me has burst to allow this understanding in. And with it, the childhood injuries suffered at my father's hands, by his alternating abuse and neglect, have been answered—answered by me, by my willingness to let the pain of loss (my own and his) in.

I think to myself, this must be the embodiment of forgiveness.

Forgiveness. It seems unfathomable that I could forgive what happened to me. People say, "Forgiveness is a decision." I gave up on that long ago, deciding that this thing called forgiveness could not possibly arise solely from the mind. And so I stopped trying to figure it out. I dug in to work on what I could change—myself.

Now I see that forgiveness is something I have given birth to—organic, visceral, of my flesh and blood, sweat and tears. And in the birthing of it I am made whole.

As I grieve the loss of my father, images of the people who have hurt me arise like needy ghosts out of the depths of my consciousness, asking forgiveness that only I can freely give. I feel the pain they must be in as though it were my own.

And I release them all to their own healing, letting go of the images of past injuries, pride and anger as they disintegrate in the gentle awareness that the perpetuation of hurt stops with me. And I release myself from the bondage of my own pain to my own healing. And I am finally home.

Lovingly
Disciplined

The lesson he's teaching appears to be...
that awakening is what happens
when we give up trying
and finally let ourselves BE.

i went to my teacher and said...

wow, like i'm really awful and i'm feeling hopeless
and i'm really tired and i just don't get it and i think i'm no good
and i'm really unhappy and i'm never gonna get it and
i wanna give it all up and go back to watching tv

and he said..... nothing

so i said.....

my discipline stinks i hardly practice i'm trying to force it but
i'm just too lazy and i end up sleeping instead i'm awful frustrated
and i get distracted and i'm always thinking 'bout sex can't i eat hot
dogs and listen to ball games

and he said..... i love you

and i said.....

i just don't deserve it i don't do like you tell me i'm always
unhappy i can't make it happen and nobody's doing it worse than i
am why should you love me, why don't you hit me, maybe i'd come
around

and he said.....

Douglas, sweet Douglas the man of so many words
to be disciplined is to do what you love and love the things that
you do   sit when you love it   stretch when you want to
pray so your feelings show thru   the disciplined fail yet fall
not from love   the problem is only in you   don't envy the others
compulsive and driven   a gentler way is for you
ouch... so many words....
come....... let's look at the view

and i said... oh...
OH!
and the beauty of the moment finally came clear

and he said..... nothing

—DOUGLAS MACINTYRE

INTENSIVE AND RETREAT EXPERIENCES

Heartwork Intensives and Retreats provide participants with the opportunity to work on their issues with the emotional and energetic support of a group. Although the issues people bring to these events are often quite varied, ultimately everyone in the group is working together toward a common goal. Because of this, the group energy created is quite powerful, and participants can do far deeper work than they can usually accomplish on their own. In addition, many personal and interpersonal issues can only be worked on when the participant is in relationship with others. Many people choose to do a combination of private work and group work, finding that each helps deepen their experience in the other venue.

Retreats emphasize the gentle, inward-looking aspects of Heartwork and tend to go "down and through" one's internal barriers to wholeness. Intensives focus on the more dynamic breakthrough potential of Heartwork, propelling participants through their fears into an experience of being totally alive and free.

These events (held on a regular basis in various locations) last from two-day "Weekend of Heartwork" events to 12-day retreats. The number of participants can vary from 20 to 50, depending on the nature of the event. You will find further information about Heartwork at the end of this book.

SONJA

Laughter and jokes hid much of our pain while growing up in our modest yellow stucco house. My father was a professional violinist, and I was very proud of him. Holding his violin case, he would walk across the living room to a chair, take his violin out and lift it gently to his chin. He might play the "Meditation" from Thais or simply act silly and play a familiar song with intermittent and laughable wrong notes. But as the pain and distance grew greater between my parents, the music in the house waned. To deal with the pain, I started to become disconnected from my true self.

My family's pain continued after I reached adulthood. I was diagnosed with breast cancer at age 44 (and had a recurrence seven years later), and my younger sister survived a heart attack. And my father, in the midst of his battle with cancer, committed suicide. Nana discovered his handwritten note on the kitchen table asking God and his family to forgive him for what he was about to do. She then found him in the back yard with a self-inflicted gunshot wound to his head. Although his brain was severely injured, his heart was still strong, and he lay unconscious in the hospital for three days before he finally died.

As a result of these horrific experiences, I remained disconnected from my self, with the denial of sorrow, anger, worthlessness and mistaken ideas lying dormant for years. Not surprisingly, my first Heartwork weekend was uncomfortable. What were these people doing, I wondered? I thought they were overreacting. I had more control. Distrusting and fearful, I did not participate fully. But I did have some powerful healing experiences.

During one exercise, I suddenly saw myself standing in Intensive Care beside my father's hospital bed, looking at his talented violinist hands now locked inside plastic bags for police evidence of gunpowder. I remembered how once those hands had made such beautiful music, and I began to sob uncontrollably. My pent-up, unresolved sorrow and grief welled up and I felt nauseated. I dry heaved periodically into a bucket for days. Emotions poured out of me until I was exhausted. In addition to grieving my father's death and the pain of not knowing his despair, I also learned that as a caring child who loved her father, I had unconsciously picked up and carried the depression of his younger years. The love and support of the group enabled me to let go of that on a deeper level. When Sunday dawned, I was a new creation. It was truly a glorious day. I was full of joy and true laughter. Day by day and layer by layer, I had confronted my grief and depression, worked through it and released it all.

The implications of this journey have had far reaching effects. For example, I recently invited my daughter to share her anger about me. I had to coax her a little because she was afraid of hurting me, but I reassured her that the experience would be healing for both of us. It was difficult to hear how I had unintentionally wounded this precious one out of my own unconsciousness and pain, but I simply listened as she spoke. After she finished each point, I urged her to tell me more, emphasizing that nothing was too small to share. When she finished, I thanked her and told her how sorry I was that I had unintentionally hurt her. I asked for her forgiveness both for what I had done and for those things I had failed to do. Later, she said that none of her friends' mothers had ever initiated or even allowed such openness and honesty. She also shared with me ways that I had supported her when no one else had. We both agreed that a shift had occurred. As difficult as that discussion was, our relationship is now more open and honest.

We may pray for peace in the world, but I have realized that peace begins with me. My only desire is to be as empty as the flute spoken of by Rumi so that God may blow his beautiful melodies through me.

BRENDA

I went to the "I and Thou" retreat alone and was partnered with a man I had never previously worked with. In the past, I would not have been open to this, but after four years of Heartwork, I have learned to trust the process. My partner seemed trustworthy and I was willing to give him the benefit of the doubt. The one thing I was certain of was that I am trustworthy and I could and would take care of myself and trust my judgment about any questionable situation that might come up. (This is not something I could have always counted on before Heartwork!)

Within a matter of two days, my partner and I had built real mutual admiration, love, and support. It's funny what can happen and how quickly it can happen when one is open. This gave me an opportunity to really delve into my deepest fears and terrors that keep me from having a relationship that I deserve and desire!

Towards the end of the third day, we did an exercise that called for one of us to lie down with our eyes closed while the other did a guided appreciation of the other. We were to take our partner's hand and arm, feel the weight, and examine how it moved. Then we were to move to the feet, then the other hand and then the head. I was thinking the purpose was to appreciate our partner and how precious life is.

But this is what occurred for me: my partner lay down first with his eyes closed, and I initially sat there, realizing that I had never touched a man other than in a sexual way. I really wanted to do the exercise and honor my partner. I wanted to express my innate love for him in an appropriate manner. So I did the first hand and I thought, "OK, this is good, I can do this." Then I went down to his feet and the thought came to me, "I'm next and I am going to have to lie there with my eyes closed." That's when the terror set in and I felt I couldn't face the situation as it was unfolding. I got really confused. I wasn't sure what would be in my best interest. Should I do something I didn't trust with someone I trusted, or should I trust that this was something I wasn't ready to do and decline to participate? Experience taught me that anticipation of the event is worse than the actual event. So even though I was scared shitless, I decided to participate.

When it was my turn, my partner did the first hand and I thought to myself, "Well this isn't so bad. Just breathe." Then he got to my foot and took my sock off to really examine my foot. I thought I was going to come unglued. As an incest survivor, I found that to lie there with my eyes closed and feel a piece of clothing come off was more than I could bear. I needed to say "Stop!" But as I did when I was a child, I immediately disassociated to be able to handle the situation and handle the terror, which meant I couldn't put my needs into words. Intellectually, I knew that I could trust this man; but emotionally, I felt as though I was a child with no choice at the mercy of her perpetrator.

At this point, I knew I had left my body and I was just trying to breathe. And I was really trying to calm down and be present. Then my partner moved to my other hand. I was getting a handle on things and calming down. I thought, "OK, I have walked through my terror, made it through to the other side. Victory is in sight!" The last part was for him to come to my head and examine it in a loving manner. So in a very sweet gesture, my partner cupped my head by putting his hands over my ears to examine my face. But then I couldn't hear. Suddenly, I was terrified again. I couldn't see, hear or speak. This is an incest survivor's nightmare. I just had to surrender and accept the fact that I did the best I could; disassociation was all I knew to do.

The next part of the exercise was to embrace your partner, feel the love you have for him or her, and express to the other person what you got from the exercise. So my partner and I faced each other, hugged and looked in each other's eyes. But the painful reality was that I had experienced so much trauma that I was numb. I really loved and trusted this man, and I couldn't feel it. It made me really sad, and I just listened to him with tears flowing from my eyes. I didn't have anything to say. I just felt how sad it was that my past had once more influenced my present. I thought about how unfair it was that I couldn't be there for my partner and how he deserved so much more. It was too much. I finally had to excuse myself to go to the bathroom so I could separate myself from the situation.

When I returned to the room, a good friend of my mine was just leaving. I could tell by the look on her face that she, too, had struggled with the exercise. She looked at me and asked, "How did it go?" I just melted into her arms and bawled. How much longer, I thought, do I have to pay for my sins? When will my past stop haunting me? Will I ever have a chance to love? I just wailed. I couldn't breathe, I couldn't see, and I didn't care who heard me! My friend just held me and then someone else (I don't know who) came and held me from behind.

When I came back into the room, we formed a circle to discuss our experiences. I sat through one after another person sharing what a loving, powerful, meaningful, sweet experience it had been. It was enough to make me sick, and I thought, "This just sucks!" So then I shared what had happened for me as I bawled. I realized that all these years I had made the decision to spare someone from having to be with such a damaged person. If I didn't expose anyone to me or my past, then I wouldn't have to face it either! It was easier not to commit, not to love, and not to be emotionally involved. Crying, I said I was tired of my past and that I was willing to surrender. I asked Dale, "How long do I have to have my past control my life?" He answered, "Would you rather be your pain or be nothing?" In my mind, I thought I would give up everything—my money, my possessions, my life—to not have the pain. I would rather be nothing! He said that our ego associates with the pain, so as long as we identify with our egos, we are going to have the pain of our past. Then he suggested we feel the pain. "Feel the depth of your pain and see where it takes you," he said. "That's your homework!"

With the help of a friend, I felt my pain that night. It was nothing compared to what was below it! Below the pain was self-hatred, and below the self-hatred was the fear that if I died (and I had been trying to kill myself all my life with my self-destructive behavior), no one would care or even notice. That was the core of my being. That was my deep well of pain and sadness. That was my worst fear. I felt my life was so insignificant that it didn't matter if I was dead or alive. How sad is that?

So much of my behavior now made sense to me. What a revelation! It sounds very hard, very painful and very uninviting. Yet this experience is one of the most powerful I have ever had in my life! I am free! Looking back, I am so grateful! I am not my abuse, and I can stop punishing myself for it and forgive myself! What my perpetrators did was nothing compared to what I have perpetuated throughout my life. In fact, I have been my worst perpetrator! But I also saw that through all the pain, the shame and the unthinkable is the GOLD—me!

ALEX

*A*t one Heartwork retreat, we did an exercise that involved working at an assigned task at one-quarter speed. My job was laying sod for a new lawn. I was skeptical, but I began to move very slowly through the task at hand. This was difficult because the slower pace gave my mind a chance to get busier, and I constantly had to catch myself, refocus on what I was doing, and slow down again.

Eventually I really got lost in the process, noticing the amazing qualities of the dirt itself and all the creatures that lived within it. I relished the feel of the moist earth *between my fingers and the degree of attention that I was bringing to the moment, really noticing the minute details. Slowing down meant that instead of working towards an end point, I was just working. I was not separate from or fighting with the task, but I was more in relationship with it and with just being. It became a meditation.*

The most important revelation I had was the simple fact that I loved working with my hands. All my life, I have made a living as a self-employed artist and craftsman, but lately I've been considering giving it up. But when I removed all the pressures of time and salability of the product I was making, I allowed myself to reconnect with the true passion that I have for what I do—a passion that had gotten lost under the business of making a living in our fast-paced, modern world.

TERESA[*]

When I was 25, I remember telling my father that I loved him and hearing him tell me for the first time that he loved me. My father is not a very expressive person when it comes to verbalizing his love, so it felt so good to finally hear these words from my daddy. Then when I was in my mid 30s, we stopped communicating after I started dating someone that he did not approve of. Yet I still wanted his love and I felt that I needed it to be whole and healthy.

While attending a Heartwork workshop, I did an exercise where people faced me and repeated, "What do you want?" I said to a man in my group who was about my father's age, "I want you to love me." He replied that he did love me, but something inside me felt that he wasn't being truthful. After a few moments, I asked him if he accepted that I loved him. After a brief hesitation, he said, "No." It felt like my heart had been ripped out. It was the most intense physical and emotional pain that I had ever felt. How could he not accept my love? In my mind, he couldn't love me if he couldn't accept that I loved him.

With Dale's help, I went deep inside that pain. He asked me where in my body I was feeling the pain and then told me to stay with it. After allowing myself to continue feeling the pain, eventually it left and I felt intense, overwhelming love. It was my love—the everlasting love within me. I then allowed myself to feel this encompassing love as completely as I could. In doing so, I was able to accept that the man in my group didn't love me, to forgive him and to love him anyway. And because this man represented my father to me, I could accept that my father didn't love me, forgive him and love him anyway. This exercise allowed me to forgive my father for our lapse in communication and I truly let go of the grievances that I had toward him. It was easy because I was in this expansive space of love.

Then, I had the courage to contact my father and tell him that I loved him, accepting the possibility that he didn't love me. And when I did, I found that he did love me. And, because I was in the glorious space of love, I could fully feel his love for me. It was overwhelming and magical, and I believe our relationship was healed forever. Even though my father may not agree with all the choices I make in the future, I know love will still dwell between us.

The pieces have been here
all your life.
Moved around the table
sliding back and forth,
some fitting,
some impossible.   Saturation
You stare and study   Point
until your eyes blur
and your head aches.
You know each piece so well.
You've studied them so long.
Until the day comes
when it's all finally enough:
the last drop is added,
or something that was forever
hard and pointed
is smoothly worn away.
From everywhere, at once,
the crystal grows its patterns:
the lace and link
of all those puzzle parts
is perfectly remade,
and last night's pain
and tomorrow's joy
find each other at last.
Like brothers and sisters,
like lovers,
like the Sun rising
on the day You,
and Everyone else,
were born.

— RICHARD WEHRMAN

TRANSFORMATIONAL LIFE STORIES

The stories in this section are those of people who not only have experienced the life-changing potential of Heartwork, but who have chosen to make it a way of life. These individuals combine private therapy work with group retreats and intensives. Their stories provide excellent illustrations of how Heartwork allows people to work on various issues with a variety of methods to find their own way home.

....

EMILY[*]

When my husband and I got divorced, I'd only experienced the numbness that emotional shock can cause one other time in my life—when I was 19 years old and my father died suddenly of a heart attack. But now, 27 years later, that numbness gripped me twice as hard as the first time. My husband had stepped out of the perfect partner/father role and had an affair with our good friend and his boss. Feeling as though I was drifting alone in a small boat out in the middle of a great sea, I mourned the loss of family and worried about the effect this would have on my teenage daughter.

The months that followed led me on a path of denial. I stopped eating and lost 45 lbs. in two months, and I cried a great deal of the time. I packed up my things into a U-Haul and along with my daughter, our cat and our dog, started a cross-country trek towards my friend's house in California. At the time, it just felt as if I was taking charge of my life and trying to survive. But I now see that full of anger, I was running from myself and the situation.

This is the point in my life when I met Dale Goldstein and was introduced to the Heartwork Institute. The first workshop I attended pushed enough of my buttons to cause me great anxiety and I bolted. Even though there was a loving approach to the intensity I was feeling, my anger came to the surface and I screamed at the well-intentioned participants to leave me alone. With that outburst, I left in the middle of the workshop at midnight in the pouring rain. My resolve was never to attend another workshop again.

However, Pandora's box had been opened and I could not stop the flow of new thinking that had started from that weekend. Eagerly, I signed up for another workshop and continued to attend them for the next three years.

At the first of these, we started off the day by picking a buddy. Another woman and I seemed to instantly gel. Others in the group picked partners, but one man who hadn't found a partner asked to join my newfound friend and me so that we could form a triad. We talked about it and decided to decline his request. Dale started our group encounter by asking me why we didn't want this man to join us. He wanted me to get up, face the man and tell him. I felt perfectly calm when I got up in the circle and faced this person. But what happened next was a complete surprise.

When I actually looked into the man's face, I suddenly felt all the hurt and anguish I'd been feeling towards my husband concerning his cheating on me. Without warning, words flew out of my mouth directed toward this man, and I let him have it. Suddenly, it wasn't the man anymore, it was my husband, and every person who had hurt me in my life, as well. I screamed at him, swore at him and released years of built-up tension.

Later, I apologized to him. By the end of the weekend our whole group had become close and bonded, sharing in a dynamic process of release and healing. Even in my darkest hour, I discovered, if I face my pain I will pass through it and into a new understanding.

Patricia D.

I remember when my grandmother was having a lot of strokes. I went with my mother to the hospital a number of times to either visit Gram or to pick her up and bring her home. Each time, as I stepped into the elevator, my fear of hospitals would begin to take hold. I felt light-headed, and I had difficulty breathing. A cold sweat broke out on my forehead while my ears began to ring. My mind reeled with thoughts about all the people who had been in that elevator on their way to see loved ones who were sick or dying.

At this time in my life, I had been practicing Heartwork in private sessions with Dale. I had several experiences in those sessions of opening to my feelings and allowing the feeling space within me to flow through me.

So standing at the foot of my grandmother's hospital bed with my siblings and my mother, I found I was in the middle of a full-blown panic attack. I took just a moment to say, "yes!" to the fear. Instead of trying to push all this fear away, I decided to let it fill me up and to allow the fear to be alive inside of me. With a swoosh, the fear-filled energy ran through my body. That was all that was needed. It lasted just a few seconds, but the experience has served me for the past 20 years because I have not experienced any anxiety going into hospitals since that time. Now that my mother is older, I've been in similar hospital settings to see her many times, but that old fear and anxiety are gone.

DONNA

I am so committed to Heartwork because in it I find courage in the face of fear and pain to go beyond the normal level of comfort and embrace the journey within. Curiosity becomes the entertainer as the endless inquiry of self satisfies its slow, forever-lengthening and broadening quest to come home. And then my eyes flicker and I am taken, transported out and within, all in one moment of pure light—the expansion of my soul's truest nature in limitless space.

Using Heartwork, I have asked myself what belief systems I adopted as a result of being abandoned by my mother and father (and so being unwanted and unloved and therefore feeling unlovable). This abandonment was proof to me that I was unlovable—that I was not nice, easily forgotten, not taken seriously and that I deserved to be ignored. My brother was the smart one, I thought—the one who would be somebody, who would go places. I, on the other hand, was a nobody, going nowhere. And if I were to manage to do something, I thought, no one would notice it anyway.

I allowed myself to be insignificant and unimportant and it hurt like hell—in fact, it still does. I allowed myself to become governed by fear, fear of the truth of who I am. At the time, I thought that the truth was hideous, so I developed my masks and characters to aid my survival. Never trusting or believing in my own self, I would believe my masks instead of the truth. I really believed my own bullshit (and in some ways, I still do).

How much do I hide behind my masks? Even when I am reflecting my true beauty, compassion and heart, my fear tells me that this goodness is only a mask to make myself acceptable, even adored and loved, and that underneath lies the rest of me—the selfish, self-centered, tired, don't-give-a-damn me.

I am proud of aspects of me and of my life, but I really don't know how to accept all of me. I am aware of all of me, but I see these parts of me as separate from each other. It's as if I can't believe that all my parts would truly make a whole that I could be proud of. I know what parts of me I like to project, yet I only allow myself complete vulnerability on very rare and special occasions. I am seeing and believing more and more of my tender side and I am allowing that to shine—or at least acknowledging that it exists.

I remain an enigma to myself; I am a living paradox. I feel whole, yet broken. Large, yet small. Happy, yet sad. Peaceful, yet chaotic. Alive, yet dead. So full, but so empty. How can I be all of these things? And how can it change in one instant to the next? How can I love myself and trust myself when I feel abandoned and betrayed? How do I even stay with myself when I feel I am fit for the refuse heap? It's not possible when my shadow is bigger than my truth in that moment.

I live LARGE, really large, then I watch myself shrink. Why is it so hard to see and accept the parts in me that I think are ugly? What is the need to be all loving and sweet and beautiful?

I long for peace, for in that peace I am love and I am loveable and able to love. The need for approval all comes back to wanting to be loved. Do I want everyone to love me? No, I don't feel that need. So who is it that I need to love me? People whom I love, whom I admire, whom I want to like me, people whom I hold in high regard. So is there a game in this for me? And how do I play it? How can I get you to like me and approve of me when I think just being me is simply not enough? If I am not enough, then you may abandon and exclude me—a double whammy.

My fear of not being good enough has held me back, made me retreat and shrink from possibilities and opportunities rather than embrace them. I have held back and held on—keeping life at arm's length. I've created walls and barriers so you can't get to me. Just look how powerful and strong I am—I'm untouchable! But it's all such bullshit, this great illusion of ME.

So if it's taken about 38 years of perfecting this belief system, then how do I change it? I want to truly change it permanently at its core. It doesn't serve me or my life—it not only detracts from my life, it actually poisons it.

I am everything and everything is all of me.

Can I be brave enough to sit with the pieces of me that I don't accept? To see and feel compassion towards myself? To see myself for who I am when I live without barriers and with the freedom I feel in that space? Maybe—in time.

It would be a truly daunting task:

to remember my own unique beauty and gifts to this world,

to remember to be present with my own life,

to remember the magic of the moment,

to remember to love and

to remember that all of God's compassion lies inside of me.

KATHARINE*

One week to the day after I completed my first Heartwork retreat, my father died. He was a charismatic, generous man with a great sense of humor, and my loss was huge—as it was for my mother and my seven siblings. Here I was with my heart wide open for the first time, grateful to Heartwork for this state of being, and a thunderbolt of staggering proportion hits the very center of our lives. Amid the chaos of funeral details, I received some sharp and unbearably painful criticism from a family member. My heart slammed shut. In an instant, I went from the most loving openness to its extreme opposite. I quickly and harshly concluded that Heartwork didn't work in the real world.

But eight years later, I can say that it has indeed made a big difference in my life in ways I didn't even anticipate. What has unfolded for me from this inner work is a life of substance. And it happened one step at a time. I began by doing a forgiveness meditation every day for three months. It seemed an appropriate place to begin because at that first retreat, I'd realized that two of my now adult children could not forgive me for my abuse to them when they were young. I actively made a commitment to have a loving relationship with both of them. When I returned and told my daughter about my plan, she said, "Mom, it has taken me 25 years to have what I do have with you. Don't try to change it now." I insisted that very night that we at least hug for the first time in years. She laughed at the very suggestion. Our A-frame hug was awkward and scary for both of us, but it was a start.

During those first three months, I not only felt compassion for myself, but I also forgave three people who broke my heart through their betrayal. Today I am free to be in their company when the opportunity arises; what I feel toward them is genuinely joyful.

My second Heartwork retreat came nine months after the first one. This event jarred me into seeing that the beliefs I held true were beginning to fracture. For instance, I saw clearly that the part of my life that was efficient, capable, organized and accountable looked toned and fit. The part that was loving, vulnerable and tender looked anorexic. I was shocked and embarrassed at this revelation. This was the antithesis of how I presented myself to others, yet somehow I knew it was true. The one blessing during those five days came during a visualization when I saw a very tender, spring-green shoot coming up from the ground. I've never forgotten that little green bud and the hopeful promise it brought me.

But soon the fractures became fragments. I didn't know what to feel or even how to feel. I didn't fit in anywhere anymore because I was learning a different language. I didn't know if I could stay in my marriage. And I had no sense of ease within myself. The more I tried to hang on to what had always worked, the more I felt lost and afraid. The ugliness of my unacknowledged self surfaced, with its covert addictions, secret longings and hidden rage. Neediness beyond anything I ever imagined became a constant companion. Outside of the other workshop participants, I couldn't tell anyone about these feelings, which led to further isolation from my husband and family.

In the earthquake of emotions, my body began to come alive. After a lifetime of no tears, I cried every day. I loved my spontaneous tears and the feeling of tenderness they engendered in my heart. It was so new to me. I also laughed more. I even laughed out loud! I realized that in more than 50 years, I had rarely given myself this pleasure. How sad is that?

A few years into my journey, I met a man at a Heartwork event who was my perfect mirror. Our lives and our families of origin were nearly perfect matches. The one difference was the strategy we used to keep from feeling our feelings. I was a people-pleaser, the "good one." People liked me. However, I would people-please until I didn't get my needs met and then I would turn to rage. He, on the other hand, was a rage-aholic, the "bad one," the one people were afraid of. He raged until he didn't get his needs met and then he turned to people-pleasing.

He and I willingly, and in a way unknowingly, joined hands and jumped into an abyss of neediness and grasping beyond description. We spent hours on the phone or in each other's company. We read books together, searching for answers. We became smug in our "enlightenment." We felt certain that we were feeding each other's souls (noble work, for sure!), but in truth, we were merely filling each other's holes. We couldn't see that while we could make the pain of our woundedness stop for a while, it always returned.

And like most drugs that anesthetize pain, the relationship quickly became an addictive hellhole. My Heartwork friend became my drug of choice.

Although at times I found great safety in his company, at other times my fear was beyond belief. I had never seen rage like his before. That kind of emotion, like tears, was not allowed when I was growing up. And I had certainly never seen my own rage. I never looked in the mirror at my own face when my volcanic temper erupted. No one knew about that dark side of me—except my kids who learned early on not to trust me and who were afraid to love me no matter how much they may have wanted to.

This whole relationship with my Heartwork friend was against societal rules. Here I was, a married woman with children and grandchildren, and all I wanted to do was run away from the life I had spent 20 years creating. I would say, "Tuscany or Thailand. Where should I go?" In truth, I didn't want to run away with him. I wanted to simply run away—most likely from myself.

My children were naturally scared when they were with me. I pontificated on the merits of Heartwork and yet lived a life that was anything but loving. And if my ground was shaking, then their ground was shaking, too. My children tried an intervention. They arranged a meeting with all of them plus my husband and me. It failed. After having spent a lifetime as the "Queen of Manipulation," I used Heartwork to defend myself and protect myself. I told them I was relentless about my work, but in truth I was ruthless. I was scared, they were scared, we all were scared. But I refused to give up Heartwork or my friend.

As my work strengthened through more Heartwork events, negatives began to fall like dominoes. My rage at perceived injustices began to melt away. Distrust in others turned to trust in myself. Honesty and integrity became necessities, and dishonesty became intolerable. Good things continued to unfold. The loneliness that victimized me for much of my life revealed itself as simply a true sadness. I know now that at times I feel sad when my heart is open. Sometimes it feels unbearable. But my personal experience is that a closed heart is even more unbearable. Through Heartwork I found that by being with the sadness and just feeling it, I felt relief and a peace within myself and with the world. No longer did I have to fill holes, run from the pain or anesthetize it. I didn't have to fix rage-aholics. I didn't have to do anything. The longing of my soul actually began to enrich my life. I still felt sadness, but I also felt tremendous joy in the smallest things. Everything began to look and feel fresh and new.

My Rolodex had to change as I discovered more of my habitual patterns. For years, I positioned myself as the one with power in relationships. I constantly sought out people who were weaker than me, more troubled than me, who needed my help or who could be manipulated into needing me. I needed people to be dependent on me. That way no one would ever leave me. And the bonus was that they thought I was wonderful. Layer upon layer of these personal truths emerged. I began to see a lifetime of withholding, invulnerability, fear and all the machinations that distanced me from others and from my feelings.

Integrating the scared little girl inside me with the grown woman I knew myself to be was difficult. But without this integration, seeing whole was impossible. And without this wholeness, the holes and emptiness would only continue to keep me imprisoned. So I signed up for a four-day Heartwork personal intensive with my Heartwork friend. I felt supported and safe at the outset. We took turns working through scary issues. Fear and anger at parents, former spouses, unknowns—you name it. Fear was the operative word. Through Dale's urging and support I was finally able to see how afraid and how abandoned the little girl inside me felt. I could see her easily, but she refused to look at me. Who could blame her? She had been abandoned for decades. But over the course of those four days she finally came to me willingly, wrapped her arms around my neck and just sat with me. This experience was so real to me that I can honestly say I felt at home for the first time in my life. And when she was sure of me being with her, she confidently led me out of the prison of my life.

In fact we trashed the prison walls together. I no longer had to go to Thailand or Tuscany. She felt safe with me. I completely trusted her and her laser insight and instinct of what was safe and what wasn't. My little girl was then able to emerge as a playful child, full of spunk and wit. Not surprisingly, I got in touch with her devout spiritual nature. She is a beautiful Child of God. I was also able to see my own devout nature and how important a spiritual path is to me. In time, I experienced a full integration of the little girl with the woman who I am. No longer were we separate identities. As the little girl felt safe, the holes disappeared, as did the loneliness and the sadness.

Fortunately for all of us, Heartwork is not about deceit, divorce and devastation of families. Heartwork is about empowering people to live the truth. Had I quit (which I wanted to do a thousand times before), had I given in to societal rules and conformity, had I not had the support of my Heartwork family and ultimately my immediate family, I feel certain I would not be enjoying the contentment that I now experience.

My relationship with my husband is now awesome. Originally, I felt my problems would be solved if only my husband would change and that all the problems in our marriage were his fault. But all that changed was me—and that changed everything. In doing work with my Heartwork friend, I saw how unapproachable I was. No wonder my husband would not open up to me. I was one scary bitch! And as much as I said in my heart that I wanted more, I withheld so much that prevented us from having any true communication. I never allowed myself to be truly vulnerable with him. We lived on the surface. We talked about the kids, the weather, work and finances, but we never talked about us. I never told him about my secret longings. I never told him I was afraid. I never told him a single truth.

As my work deepened, I could ease into conversations and soften when I sensed his fear. I experienced tremendous sadness at times that the man I shared my life with was afraid of me. And realizing that we spent so many years withholding our love, joy and truth was a bitter pill to swallow. At times, it was all I could do not to run away. One time I sat in my room for four days observing the struggle of ego. I did not speak to my husband during that time. I knew it was my issue, not his, and any words from me would be spiteful and venomous. My ego had taken a direct hit, and rather than attack him because I felt I was right and he was wrong, I just sat with the struggle in my mind. Eventually I was able to tell him of my intense conflict coming to grips with all this, and as I softened, he softened, as well.

I found that I didn't really need him to change. I just needed to be heard. And I needed him to understand that this work is hard and that I was doing the best I could not to blame him any longer. When he heard me, he reached out and held my hand, and the struggle between us just stopped—no more wars fought with the silent treatment, no withholding, no fear. We both relaxed into the relationship. Now, we often just look at each other and laugh hysterically about the simplest thing. We feel so free to be real that we can even get pretty silly sometimes. After 25 years of marriage, seven children and many years of allowing fear to dictate our actions, we can now truly enjoy the pleasure of each other's friendship. Does that mean we never have problems? Hell no! But I have the Heartwork tools to deal with my feelings and reactions in a healthy way, and I admit to myself and to him when I'm struggling.

My relationship with my children is not only healing, but it's also becoming more honest, open and loving. It is much easier to be open when you have nothing to hide. I put all my faults out in public for them. I openly and willingly claim all the wrongs, hurts and past transgressions. The very act frees me further. I ask for them to call me on my stuff. I want my unconscious behavior to stop. I want to do no harm. I want to just love them without all the judgments and all the rote expectations that society has inflicted on us all.

My children and I have even attended several Heartwork events together (and last summer, my husband also came to a family intensive). We are learning how beautiful and freeing the truth is. We are not without our problems, and painful disconnections still occur. But clean, compassionate and caring intentions are changing our family dynamic. Sharing tears of joy and tears of sadness are becoming more commonplace. This is the legacy I want for my children and my grandchildren.

My daughter, who before didn't want a real relationship with me, is a constant joy in my life. I can clearly understand her previous reluctance. And truthfully, I never could outwit her anyway. She saw through my every manipulation. Usually, she called me on it, even as a young child. Today what we enjoy is outrageously honest and respectful. We talk on the phone every day and love our time together when we get it.

I feel tremendous softness in my heart for my son, who received the brunt of my rage. I know in time he will have the courage to love me without hesitation. My intention as well as my love for him remains strong. We both deserve a loving relationship with each other. We both just want to be loved.

My Heartwork friend is still in my life. We continue to share books and thoughts and curiosities about the work. But we don't talk daily anymore. Now our connections have a more natural flow. No longer are we scared little kids dependent on each other. No longer are we trying to fix ourselves or each other. Mostly we just allow. We are amazingly caring and courageous adults committed to loving relationships within our inner circles.

My years of struggling in the quicksand of the ego have been worth it. Thanks to Heartwork I have found that there is no life without conscious awareness and truth. Yet I am also aware that this is a never-ending journey. And so my work and my growth continue.

Robert*

*W*hen I first started doing Heartwork, my life was a mess, inside and out. I had always excelled at staying on top of things and living what many would call an exemplary life. I also considered myself healthy in mind and spirit. But all of that got stripped away as I heroically devoted myself to helping a very troubled person who seemed to require every ounce of my heart and soul to keep from self destructing or potentially turning on me. Over the course of several years, this tumultuous relationship eroded all my boundaries and took possession of my life. I was in quicksand. Trying to get both of us to the solid ground of sanity proved impossible—the shore always receded* at the same rate we "progressed" through layer after layer of her distress. Any struggle to differentiate myself aroused her anxieties and inevitably pulled me in deeper. By the time I finally knew I had to struggle loose on my own, come what may, I barely had a self left. I felt like a quivering puddle of protoplasm.

I was unsuccessfully trying to recover from this state in individual psychotherapy when I met Dale Goldstein. He quickly earned my trust and invited me to my first Heartwork Basic Intensive—a four-day group process of healing, release and coming alive. Thus began for me an eight-year experience of deep healing and transformative personal and spiritual growth.

I now realize that an emotional crash of this magnitude was the only way to rupture the ego defenses that I had spent my life so carefully erecting. And into those breaches flowed the healing balm of Heartwork, to call forth and empower the soul that I buried and left for dead since my early childhood.

As I lay on the floor early in the weekend of this first intensive, I began releasing my tattered defenses and opening to love. The whole group spontaneously made a circle around me, lifted me off the floor in unison and gently rocked me. As I allowed the love to begin flowing into depths that had never felt love before, my tears began to release the walls of fear, inadequacy and autonomy that had separated me from other people and from my own soul for so long. This was my first step towards wholeness—a reuniting with my body and soul.

Another step came a little later when I was again lying on the floor. I showed Dale the place in my gut that held the knot of pain I was carrying—from both my traumatic experience as well as from years of separation from myself. Dale care-fully pinched the exact point in my gut so that the level of physical pain on the outside matched the level of emotional pain on the inside. This opened a door, and I was able to release the inner pain physically and emotionally.

Another exercise got me in touch with the feeling of utter powerlessness I had experienced during my previous relationship when I felt I was descending into quicksand, which then took me back to the sense of powerlessness I had as a frequently hungry infant. (My mother followed the doctor's orders to breastfeed me only every four hours, in spite of my crying.) That and our difficulty in emotionally connecting in childhood had caused me to draw into myself, mistrust other people and bury virtually all of my feelings. Emotionally and physically reconnecting to that powerlessness and loneliness helped me further reclaim my lost soul and integrate it into myself. I experienced a sense of wholeness down to the depths of my belly.

As a result of these experiences, I have not only been living with a much fuller feeling of who I am, but I also resonate with people emotionally at a much fuller level. I can claim my own power, open my heart to pain and to joy, and live in a state of peace and wholeness most of the time.

My two most recent Heartwork experiences were eight-day and ten-day Heartwork retreats, about three years apart. These retreats have helped me more fully let go of the barriers that keep emerging between my head and my heart. They've also helped me "go out of my mind" and into the present moment, with my ego receding into the background and even disappearing for spans of time.

I participated in the ten-day retreat from the comfort and distractions of my own home and work via conference calls and individual exercises. Early in the retreat, an agitated energy entered my awareness that was like a fish flopping around out of water, never slowing down. "What is this?" I wondered, and then I realized it was the energy that keeps my brain flipping from one thing to the next when I try to do everything and am present to nothing. So I opened my awareness to this energy and absorbed it as fully as I could. In a few minutes, it had dissipated—"metabolized" by awareness, as Dale says. And though I have had a packed schedule much of the time since the retreat, that agitated energy has never returned. I am busy, but not driven by this compulsive, anxious energy.

At one point during the retreat I felt stuck on a plateau, so I used the "What do you want?" exercise, going more and more deeply into my essential Self and its deep longings. I quickly got in touch with what I deeply want, which is to be fully alive and awake to all of life's textures, contours and poignancy. I then asked, "What is keeping me from this?" I began getting in touch with early adolescent feelings of awkwardness, ineptness and loneliness, which no doubt fuel my compulsive quest for competence. Opening my inner awareness, I experienced memories of times when I had felt ashamed, guilty, rejected and alone. I saw a picture of my face corresponding to each memory, all from different stages of my life. After holding them all in awareness, I began drawing them into my heart one by one, welcoming them all back into myself so that they could be a part of me rather than a part of my shadow. Afterward, I felt incredibly whole, energized and light. Though still on retreat, I was scheduled to help lead a meeting that evening that dealt with a controversial issue. I immediately knew how I would facilitate it and was eager to jump right in—totally free from the usual anxiety I feel when I enter conflicted situations. The next day, I took my newly found "lost boys" out for a romp in a park, and we had the best time experiencing and responding to the world through child-like energy full of curiosity, wonder and exuberance.

Through experiences like these, and through daily meditation in which I practice awareness and "losing my (egoic) mind," I find myself carrying less stress and strain. I'm growing in my sense of presence, no matter what I'm doing. All of my experiences with Heartwork have combined with my own spiritual practices to open me to the life energy that flows through me, to help me connect deeply with other people, to know and keep appropriate boundaries and to be much more responsive to the needs of my body, emotions and spirit. Heartwork for me has not been a set of exercises, experiences or tools as much as it's been an ongoing path of deeply opening to life itself.

Patricia T.

My journey to healing through Heartwork began more than a dozen years ago. After thoughts of suicide and many years of individual as well as group therapy, I continued to struggle with feelings of anger, fear, insecurity and a deep unexplainable longing. What I knew for sure was that typical fifty-minute therapy sessions were not working for me. My pain was profound, my shame too great, and my ability to trust so broken that no amount of fifty-minute sessions would allow me to experience the healing for which I longed.

When I met Dale—who was conducting four-hour personal intensives on back-to-back days—I felt that at last I had found someone whose approach might work for me. Although my life appeared to be successful on the outside, on the inside I was living in a self-created hell, and the well of pain I had been living with since I was 14 had only gotten deeper.

I approached that first personal intensive with great fear mixed with anger and emotional pain. This manifested as a feeling of hot, boiling lava inside my gut. After the first session, I could feel that the amount of "hot lava" had lessened. Although I had hope, I was still afraid of how much lava was left and was not confident I could get it all out. On the second day, I let go and found myself kneeling on the floor of Dale's office, dry-heaving and gagging into a bucket as the hot lava of my emotional pain spewed forth. Dale's compassionate presence gave me the courage to tell my story and made me feel that I was never alone. He shared every word and every tear of my journey. After more than 30 years I had finally met a man I could trust.

My most recent experience with Heartwork was the "Letting Go" retreat. This ten-day combination of meditation, exercises, personal sessions and bodywork was one of the best things I have ever done for myself. Although I began the retreat feeling very anxious, I was committed to giving it my all because I knew it would take me to the next level in my healing journey.

My intention for the retreat was to reconnect with my body. I had disconnected from it during my teens in order to cope with sexual and physical abuse. Like all survival defenses, it worked for me then, but later in life it started working against me—manifesting itself as emotional pain in parts of my body that kept me from feeling free. In particular, my bladder would frequently spasm, causing me such discomfort that I sought medical help and took prescription drugs. When that wasn't successful, I went through lengthy biofeedback treatments. None of that offered permanent relief because none of it addressed the cause of the problem, which was emotional rather than physical. As I continued the retreat, I learned that my body had actually stored the sexual abuse in my bladder.

My bladder problem was so severe that by merely walking past a bathroom, I would get an uncontrollable urge to go. And going out in public required that upon entering a new store or restaurant, I immediately would have to locate the restroom because I had to go about every hour. Because the bladder stores toxins, I had to face the painful reality that the disconnection that I had created in order to survive sexual abuse had turned my body into a toxic waste dump. And a body that is a toxic waste dump isn't a safe place to be. As I owned this as my truth, I had to face the reality that I had passed this on to my daughter, who was diagnosed with asymptomatic, chronic urinary tract infections at age seven and wet the bed until she reached her teens. Is there scientific evidence to prove this? Of course not. I only know that it resonates as absolute truth with me. And when I look back at my past, it offers the only plausible explanation for much of my experience and for the experience of my daughter.

No matter how hard I tried, my "little girl" hadn't wanted to stay in my body—she just continued to run away, making it impossible for me to stay present during meditation and during life. But through his compassion and support, Dale stayed present with me, gave me the courage to feel the pain and loved me into healing.

When I shared this truth about myself with him, I learned that he still accepted and loved me. If he could still love me, how could I not love myself? He gave me a place to put the pain so I no longer had to carry it. He taught me that through soft body and awareness meditation and staying present, my body could evolve from a toxic waste dump into a place of peaceful connection.

Because of practicing Heartwork I am forever changed.

LOUELLA*

*M*y doctor recommended that I see Dale because he noticed that I was becoming anxious and he was aware that I had bouts with depression. I did not want to start seeing a therapist and was rather angry that he was asking me to do so. Dale has a policy to call all his referrals, so when I received his call, I decided to go to one appointment.

When I first met Dale, I was angry and not ready to be cooperative. I felt defensive and I had no plans to return. During the course of the first session, I broke down while explaining the frustration and anger I was having in my life. I felt overwhelmed, lonely and unappreciated. Once I admitted these feelings, I cried for the first time in years. When I looked up, Dale was grinning from ear to ear. He said that I was in an existential crisis and that he could help me. I couldn't remember ever asking for help in my life, and it was hard to remember very many people ever saying they could actually help me. So I decided to continue private sessions.

At the time, I was having such frequent and intense panic attacks that I had considered suicide as an escape. When I wasn't in panic, I was usually in depression or despair. I was on the defensive all the time. My job was miserable and I had turned my back on all the possibilities of life. I had become cynical, defensive, tired and lifeless. I made my world very small and "safe," but joyless and lonely.

For the first five months, I saw Dale weekly. During that time, I committed to a daily meditation practice and read books that Dale recommended, such as When Things Fall Apart by Pema Chodron and Siddhartha by Hermann Hesse. Suppressed childhood memories began to surface. Deep longing and the sadness of my desperately lonely and fearful childhood came on quite intensely. Although Dale was attentive and caring, I became more defensive and deeply frustrated. The fight had begun. It took me years to get clarity on what was happening for me in those first few months of this work.

I wanted Dale to be my mother and I wanted to know what it was like to have a loving, kind and interested father. I knew he would be very good at filling both of those roles, and I became very attached to him. I hid my "bad" self and tried to convince him of how loveable, wonderful and beautiful I could be. I was intensely afraid of being rejected, misunderstood and left out. The basis of Heartwork is to become whole within ourselves—to be our own mother (nurturer) and our own father (protector). But that seemed too frightening, and I was very fearful that I was not ever going to be able to do that for myself. All my fears of abandonment and rejection came flooding in.

Because Dale absolutely refused to give me what I wanted, I reverted back to being a very frustrated child. I became afraid of showing my pain to him because I felt I was too vulnerable, so I went on high alert. I watched everything I said and did. I braced myself for every blow. I attacked first to try to keep some kind of control over my pain. I lost all sense of my truth and my needs. I had very little trust in myself. I constantly watched Dale for cues on how I should behave. I had essentially recreated my childhood and was acting the way I needed to act to survive in my family and community. I had handed over my power to Dale because I needed something from him and cared too much about what he thought about me and because I desperately wanted him to be my father.

Dale encouraged me to feel the pain and suffering of my predicament. I started doing a great deal of very deep grieving for all the loss and feeling the sheer frustration of not being able to get what I wanted from him (which was really the grief of never getting what I needed from my parents). Childhood grief and fear hardened into anger. I needed him to see me and how hurt I was. Many months went by before I could start pulling away the wall I had built around my heart.

I began to realize that this suffering served me because I needed to go back and experience the pain and fears of childhood that I had suppressed and that still had a tremendous hold on me. Dale spent a great deal of time encouraging me to go inside and see who was so hurt and to ask her what she needed. We did Guided Heartwork meditations to go into the places that were hurting. He asked me to become aware of when I abandon myself. It was very difficult for me to stay focused inside and on the feelings that were coming up. It was very easy for me to go to my "story" and simply play it over and over, hoping I could change the story or get something from him rather than staying with the deep feelings. I needed to allow my heart to break open without any interference or protection from Dale or anyone else. What Dale knew that I didn't know then was that care-taking actually disempowers people and prohibits growth and healing.

After a few months, I decided to attend a Heartwork weekend. The group work brought up tremendous pain and fear for me and I had a very difficult time processing it. I began reacting to everything and I became very angry. I was very confused and lost my sense of reality. Since I was prone to abandon myself quite rapidly and since I did not trust my own inner experience, I was left vulnerable to the group. Everyone's stuff was getting in and twisting me around pretty good. I had become hypersensitive to just about everything. My inner critic really started beating the heck out of me.

Dale calls the critic our caged gorilla. He told me to let the gorilla beat me up and just surrender to it. He asked me to look into the gorilla's eyes and to tell him what I saw.

I saw tremendous sadness, loneliness and despair. I actually started having compassion for the gorilla. One time he asked me to imagine what it would be like if the gorilla were to leave the cage that we were in together. I immediately became very frightened and realized I would be very lonely. I would have had to feel the fear of abandonment. I realized that I would rather be mistreated non-stop by my gorilla-critic than face the fact that I am alone. I feared abandonment and my ultimate death so much that I created this "companion." This discovery provided the clarity I needed to finally make friends with that part of myself, and I knew I would not be able to go deeper into this work or transcend the suffering without this piece.

Eventually, I actually sat down and had a conversation with my critic. I thanked her for being there for me all those times I needed her. I apologized to her for trying to get rid of her and I had compassion for how frightening that must have been. I explained to her that she had gone too far and that I needed her to back off and go into retirement. My critic doesn't have a hold on me anymore, and I am much less reactive. I am much more present for myself. I have the space and clarity I need.

My heart opened more and more through the years as my inner process continued. I came to accept that I did not have control over much of what I saw and experienced, but that I needed to go back into the despair and be there for myself. I began doing what I never could have even imagined when I started working with Dale. I consoled myself. And even though I had made great strides, I sometimes found myself sliding backward. But those setbacks proved to be wonderful places for growth.

During a recent retreat, doing the Inward Bend exercise taught me that fighting the pain or wishing the pain would go away made it much worse. Letting go into the pain changed everything. It took a lot of practice and commitment to allow that experience to take root and to take on the meaning that could facilitate life change: pushing anything away or denying anything just made it become bigger.

I also found that as I leaned into the questions of Inquiry, or noticed my sequence of reactions and felt them moment to moment with Freeze Frame, I could see in excruciating detail how I betrayed myself and how that felt. The more I inquired into and froze those reactions, the more I learned how to stand up for myself. Inquiry kept my judgments in check, while Freeze Frame became my teacher and guide.

One of my realizations was that I had made my world so "safe" that I was afraid to take even the simplest risks. Dale was steadfast in encouraging me to make my own choices. He absolutely would not do it for me. I needed to sit in the discomfort of not knowing what to do. I inquired into it and found that I am truly the only person I can completely trust. I began to take a few risks and found that once I had learned to love myself directly, I no longer needed to impress others.

As I have grown, it has been more difficult for me to be involved in anything that is not aligned with my integrity—including the activities I had created during times of self-abandonment and low self-esteem. So almost two years ago, I took what I considered to be a giant risk and quit a job that was draining my energy, stifling my creativity and damaging my self-esteem. Instead, I stayed at home with myself to heal and do Heartwork full-time. Initially this decision scared me because I had lots of bills and hardly any savings. But I knew I had to break this destructive cycle. I decided to trust that the Universe could hold me while I took the time to nurture myself and heal the wounds that kept me from having what I wanted and deserved in life. For about four months, I allowed myself the space to regroup and prepare to make the changes I wanted.

Choosing a new direction created tremendous anxiety, partly because I felt I had so much to offer that I wanted to do it all. But doing it all is impossible, and wanting that paralyzed me. I discovered that I enjoyed many things and that if I did any one of them, I could make a nice living. The bottom line was that I had been asking the wrong question! The key wasn't finding what I wanted to do, but rather how I wanted to be. More specifically, I needed to ask myself, "How do I want to be treated (by myself and by others) and how do I want to be remembered?" I found that my job itself wasn't ever what was dissatisfying. It was working with people who used me as their personal punching bag and allowing them to treat me that way.

As a result, I decided to move from being an expense (that needs to be controlled and reduced) on an employer's profit and loss statement to being an asset that will not only be appreciated but that will also appreciate in value. I started my own accounting practice, which I run from my home office. When I was an expense, I believed my employers when they told me I had to do more for less, that I wasn't worth investing in, and that I could be easily replaced. But once I saw myself as an asset, I instantly experienced a paradigm shift. As I would with any other asset, I now want to keep myself in good running order to increase my value and my useful life. I no longer feel repressed, tired, cynical and defeated. I now feel free to bestow my gifts upon all who know they deserve what I have to offer. And not surprisingly, I expect to earn at least five times what I earned at my last job, even including benefits. I also feel the freedom that comes from loving and respecting myself—without thinking that I have to look outside myself for that validation. That's something that's worth more than any paycheck or benefits package!

MARY JANE

*W*hen I first learned about Heartwork, it had been a little more than two years since I left my husband, whom I still consider my soul mate. I kept replaying the tapes of our final months in my mind, looking for ways I could have changed the outcome. Longing for my soul mate was the deepest pain I had ever felt. But I knew my life had to change, so once I began doing Heartwork, I committed to giving it my all. At the time, I felt my mind was at stake. What I came to realize was that my soul was at stake!

In my first Heartwork session, Dale told me I could not control or run from the demons in my head, and he asked me if I was willing to face them. As I closed my eyes, I saw an endless swirling black mass with flashes of neon yellow, orange and red. It hurt my eyes and I wanted to run away, but Dale encouraged me to stay and face my pain. Soon the flashes stopped, but I still felt a heavy weight in my chest. I went into the pain, allowing myself to face this black mass. It felt as though I was going into a dark, foreign cave. It was terrifying! With barely enough light to see, I commanded myself to keep going. I smelled noxious fumes and heard eerie noises, and I warily kept watch for bats and whatever else might be lying in wait for me. Gradually, it got lighter, and finally at the end I found an infant child—a beautiful baby, all by herself, with her arms reaching up to me. I picked her up, held her and comforted her, and my heart burst with love. The heavy mass was gone from my chest. I knew who this baby was—my infant self, my unloved little girl. This was the unwanted child who was never good enough, who was abandoned at birth by her mother, abandoned again at 13 months by her grandmother, and then abandoned by me as an adult over and over again in my search for love and acceptance.

The sharp pains I'd been feeling in my chest disappeared after my initial experience with Heartwork, so I was eager to explore my issues more fully. I had been plagued with chronic pain for years, and I had tried many different medications along with various surgeries, therapies and different types of doctors to no avail. I hated my lack of mobility and my powerlessness! Dale suggested that every time I felt pain I calmly and curiously go into it, asking, "What is this?" to see what might come up. It seemed hard to believe that all my physical problems could be emotional in nature, but I was sure willing to see how many I could get rid of, just in case that was true.

I learned that if I was not assertive about my feelings and internalized them, they would manifest physically. Once, for example, I felt a tense ache across my neck and blamed it on too much computer work. But when I went into the pain and inquired what it was about, I found my brother, who is often a "pain in the neck." I had been really *angry at him for about a week and was holding on to a big resentment. I couldn't believe the size of that feeling! While I meditated on it, I also realized I missed the closeness we had as children. He was not the brother I had as a child; we no longer had that kind of tight, loyal relationship, and I missed it. So I felt grief there, as well. I decided to forgive him and tell him that I still loved him. After I e-mailed him those sentiments, the pain disappeared.*

I next attended a Heartwork forgiveness retreat, where I kept coming back to the loss of my marriage and the mistake I made by leaving it. It became more and more obvious to me that I needed to forgive myself for making the choices I did. I eventually started to realize that I had brought pain on myself as a way of getting others (especially my mother and my husband) to give me the love and attention that I needed. That seemed pathetic to me, but I reminded myself that it wasn't the capable adult woman I was today who needed that love and attention—it was the abandoned little girl inside me. And she needed my help so I could stop this cycle.

My first experience at the retreat with Circular Breathing felt like giving birth, and I thought maybe I was giving birth to some new freedom. As I lay on the floor breathing deeply, my buddy pressed on my sternum (which was so painful I thought I would pass out) and kept encouraging me to breathe. Out of the pain, terror and spiraling blackness came tears and screaming. I was afraid and angry and cried for my mother. Then I cried at my mother, "I hate you! I hate you!" Then I wanted my grandmother and felt this rage because my mother had sent her away. I could see my grandmother rocking me when I was a baby, fixing me a special breakfast at her little house, showing me how to braid rugs, and always holding me and loving me and telling me I was special. Defining my original wound as the loss of my grandmother was a defining moment.

Then we did Freeze Frame, and I chose a buddy I had never worked with before simply because our eyes met across the room. In this exercise, she was to play my mother. What a coincidence that she looked like my mother did when I was a child! We faced each other and I closed my eyes and recalled that moment when my mother returned after spending 13 months in rehab from polio. She was 34 years old and married to a struggling dairy farmer. Her 60-plus-year-old mother-in-law had been taking care of her children while she was away, and the two women agreed about almost nothing. I was 13 months old, bow-legged and dressed in the fashion of children my grandmother had last raised in 1910. My mother had not seen any of her three children in those 13 months, and I had always been told that when she saw me, she wanted to go back to the hospital. I imagined my mother walking into her kitchen with her canes. My dad stood protectively behind her, looking a little lost and overwhelmed. We three children, ages four, two and one, stood facing her alongside my grandmother, who looked stern and defensive.

At that point we froze the action, and I opened my eyes, looking directly into my buddy's eyes. I saw compassion, love, tears and pain. I didn't see a woman who was horrified by her youngest child. I saw a woman who felt guilty for having left her children in the care of someone whose parenting she didn't respect. I saw a woman who was saddened that her illness affected her children. And I saw a frightened woman who wondered how she would ever care for three children and a husband and manage a household while being handicapped. I saw a woman who felt overwhelmed and lost. I felt compassion and forgiveness for this woman who had lost her own mother at a very young age. I felt love and caring for this woman who had no family of her own living near her, only her husband's family, who didn't really accept this "city girl." I understood that her heart had probably closed part way when her mother died, and that it finished closing during the 13 months she spent in the invasive horror of polio wards. I accepted that her failure to show me the love and affection that I wanted and needed did not come from an absence of love but from a closed heart. I put my arms around my buddy, and she embraced me, and I believe my mother felt that embrace because I felt hers through my buddy.

During the rest of the exercise, I needed to go into my mother's pain, take it on and acknowledge that I had created and perpetuated a lie for more than 50 years. The lie was that my mean and miserable mother had sent my wonderful grandmother away. I had made my mother the villain, I realized, because if my grandmother had simply left on her own, that would have meant something was really wrong with me. My mother's narcissism combined with her closed heart had helped perpetuate the belief that she was the evil one, and of course my grandmother was glad to let me believe she was my hero. Now, with the help of my buddy, I was able to ask my mother for forgiveness and begin the process of giving up my victim role.

I could remember getting affection from my mother when I was sick or hurt. I was always falling down as a child, and I was told I was clumsy and not careful. But now I could clearly see that this was the beginning of my hurting myself in order to be loved and nurtured—a pattern that would follow me all my life. Several months before, my ex-husband suggested that perhaps I had created the lump in my breast that I was so worried about as a means to get his attention and affection. I had been hysterical with worry over the lump, but he saw it as manipulation. I was furious! The lump turned out to be nothing. After this exercise, I wanted to examine that, and when I did, I found a clear pattern of illness and injury that included several surgeries—and with each one,

I'd received a major amount of love and kindness from my mate. I was ready to give up this pattern and learn to be loving and nurturing to myself daily so I wouldn't have to look for it elsewhere.

When I later attended a Heartwork Intensive, another Circular Breathing exercise found me walking on a road, while my buddy pressed on my sternum and encouraged me to breathe. My ex-husband was along the side of the road, a strong, comforting presence. Down the road, I saw a light and I knew I should go forward, but doing so would require that I leave his side, and that seemed too frightening. As I tried to move forward, my stomach was in knots and I was terrified at the thought of walking into the unknown without his support. When I finally did walk down the road, I found my infant self in a lovely meadow. She was beautiful and perfect and reminded me of my granddaughter. I felt loving and protective toward her and took her in my arms, held her, rocked her and told her she was home. Finding her was an affirmation that I needed to walk away from my ex-husband, to let him go. I didn't need him; I had my little girl self.

I asked the other two members of my group to do the circular breathing with me again a few days later. As I lay on the floor, one pressed on my sternum as the other two held my hands, encouraging me. "You can let go of him," they told me. "You are not alone." I walked a bit further up the road. My stomach cramped, and tears streamed down my face. As I walked away from my ex-husband, I felt like my heart was being wrenched from my body. "You are loved," they said. "You are strong. Keep going." I was so frightened. How would I live without him? How would I manage on my own? "You are a strong woman!" they told me. I walked slowly toward the light at the end of the road and found a cliff! Now what, I wondered? I was in a panic. I wanted to run back to him where it was safe and cry, "Protect me! Help me! Save me! Fix me!" But my group said to me, "Go ahead, Mary Jane!"

Go ahead? Were they crazy? I couldn't see what was over the edge of the cliff! It was completely black! "Jump, Mary Jane!" they said. "You can fly!" Dale had asked us to think of a song of joy, and what my group didn't know was that the refrain of my song was, "Why walk when you can fly?" I knew when I heard them tell me that I could fly that indeed, I could. And so I launched myself off the cliff and floated slowly down and deeper into the dark. As I continued to breathe, it got lighter and I floated into a brilliant meadow where my little girl waited. She stood with her arms raised, cheering for me and loving me unconditionally.

I now understood that my ex-husband represented the love and nurturing that my little girl never got from her mother. Whenever I was most needy, when I missed him the most, was when I was not feeling well or needed some kind of support. I was learning to pay loving attention to my little girl and to give her what she wanted and needed. My supreme codependency and people pleasing came from a childhood struggle to find love and affection—but it had meant abandoning my own self again and again.

Willing to keep doing the work, I next attended the Letting Go retreat. As the retreat began, I struggled with being able to focus, so I asked myself, "What am I running from? What am I afraid of?" The answer wasn't a good one: "I am flawed and my mother was right not to want me." But I knew that that was not the truth about my mother anymore. I meditated again and saw a wall, which dissolved into legs. One leg had a brace (representing my mother). This became the legs of all the people who have been critical of me (including my brother, my husbands and my supervisors at work)—everyone who said I wasn't good enough. It became thicker and thicker with people who said, "You don't deserve to know the truth of who you are!" I felt despair and loss and heard a very small voice say, "It's not true. I do deserve," but the wall wouldn't budge.

Frustrated, I went outside. It was warm and sunny, and I sat on the grass above the river, breathing the clean air, listening to the birds and insects and smelling autumn. I was totally present, and I stretched out on the grass, getting an ant's-eye view of the world. "I am one with the universe! I am a child of the universe!" I thought to myself. I had the same joyful feeling as a child when I would swing on the huge old tree by our house. I would sing as I pumped myself higher and higher on the swing, my feet reaching out and kicking the leaves as I flew forward! It was exhilarating! I felt like I could fly! And I knew I was a child of God!

Filled with this feeling, I meditated again on the wall of legs that was now so thick I couldn't see the end of it. I said to the wall, "Get out of my way. I am a child of the universe, and we are one!" And the legs dissolved.

And so, strong and courageous, I continue my journey…

SARAH[*]

*D*uring the initial sharing at the weekend Heartwork Intensive, I felt an increasing tightness in my chest, and I told the group that I wanted to get rid of it. Dale said, "We can't get rid of something by trying to get rid of it. It's a part of us, and we can't deal with it by disowning it. Whatever the pain, there's tremendous power in going into it, being with it, fully experiencing it. Then release comes on its own—without us doing anything. Doing comes from the will, so we can't 'do it.' It's a paradox."

In the afternoon, the pressure of emotions continued to build inside me. I told Dale that I wanted help moving through what I was feeling. I stretched out on my back on the floor and closed my eyes. The others in the group put their hands on me, and I felt surrounded by love.

"What do you see?" Dale asked.

"I see light."

"See if you can fill your whole being with that light."

I saw and felt the light expand within me. But when the light reached my chest, it collided with a wall of tightness. I felt my body tremble, then explode into deep, convulsive sobs.

"It's stuck—it won't go any further," I said through my tears.

"It's O.K. We'll get through it," Dale reassured me. "Can you describe what that tightness feels like?"

"It feels like a brick lying across the whole inside of my chest."

"Let yourself go into that brick and be totally with it."

I sunk into the brick, deeper, deeper—and into the pain of that tightness. Even in the midst of that pain, I was aware of the love surrounding me. That love was the ever-present reminder that my pain was not the ultimate reality, and it gave me the courage to keep going deeper into the pain. As I continued to be with the pain, the brick gradually dissolved. Across the inside of my chest where the brick had been, a tiny puppy lay in frozen stillness.

"What does that puppy need?" Dale asked, and I felt my heart open.

"It wants to be loved," I answered.

I stroked the puppy and sent it love. Bravely, it opened first one eye, then the other. Before long, it started wagging its tail and licking my face. Then it jumped up and scampered off to play—and my "little girl self" ran joyfully after it. With deep, expansive breaths, I felt my chest open up—and let go of its years of holding. I smiled, thinking of how I'd wanted to get rid of the tightness. That "brick" had been a part of me—a buried vault of pain. When I allowed myself to go into that pain, the blocked energy released on its own.

Then I began to have flashes of the trauma that had created the energy blocks. I relived the terror and isolation that I'd known as a little girl: being left alone in my crib, rarely held, beaten and raged at by my mother. I experienced again the fear and confusion that I felt when my mother was in and out of mental hospitals, and my father turned more and more to alcohol to keep from feeling his pain. With each step on this journey of non-avoidance, Dale guided me with loving persistence into facing and being with the pain.

After releasing years of pain around my mother, I found myself viewing what had happened from her perspective—and feeling her pain and terror. I saw myself hugging her, and we were crying together. I sent her love and felt my heart open up in forgiveness. With the healing of these old wounds, I experienced a wonderful sense of relief and freedom.

Later that day, I began talking about this thing that I'd sensed as a dense, dark gray blob surrounding my oldest daughter. After she had been raped at the age of seventeen, a darkness seemed to overtake and possess her. During the months that followed, she sank deeper into depression and illness. Dale encouraged me to take a deeper look at what I had sensed. Frantically, I tried to talk Dale out of this ridiculous idea.

"I don't know what you'll find in there," he replied, "but I do know that it will be beautiful." I wasn't convinced. "Whatever you find inside there," he added, "I can tell you that it'll be a whole lot better than where you are now."

So...in I went. I felt as if I were going into the contents of a giant vacuum cleaner bag—gray and vile and choking. Then it developed a monster face and fangs and claws, and I felt engulfed in terror. Dale leaned in close and kept whispering, "Stay with it, be with it." My arms flew up and grabbed him. I felt as if I'd turned into a blob of jelly, but somehow, I did manage to stay with it.

After a while, Dale asked me what the gray monster thing needed, and I thought, "This, too? Why love, of course!" Then I actually felt my heart open a bit to this monster blob. I sent it love. I began wondering, "Is even this a part of me?" At some point, the fangs and claws disappeared. Gradually, the gray blob became smaller and less dense, and it developed a misty quality. Then something made me reach my hand through the gray into its center, and when I pulled my hand out, I was holding an amethyst—and the gray blob was gone. Then, suddenly, I found the amethyst inside me, in the very center of my body, sending out its beautiful violet rays. The group of loving people around me said that I was glowing.

After the intensive, my guts were churning. The process had taken off on its own— releasing old fear and energy blocks. I knew that the only thing to do was to allow it to happen, and to stay with it. Sometimes I felt a little panicky without Dale and Ellen and the group around for support. But I know that I can be with all of it—even the panic. If I've learned anything, it's to feel what's there, and not to run from it. I can get support when I need it; but I can also be alone with myself. Whenever I go inside myself, I know immediately that I'm not alone.

As I progressed through my inner work, I realized that the gray monster encompassed much more than the darkness around my daughter. The monster was also the cloud of despair with which I'd struggled in recent years. With the break-up of my marriage, my daughter's continuing illness, and her having to give up a baby for adoption that she'd had after a brief relationship, I've often felt overwhelmed by pain and tragedy and by the extreme demands on my energy. At times, it took far more courage for me to face living each day than to face dying. But since the Intensive, I felt a sense of readiness to take on whatever challenges life presents.

Two months later, I attended another Heartwork Intensive. Exactly a week before, I'd gotten a letter telling me what I already knew in my gut: I had not gotten a job that had seemed like it would be the answer to my prayers. When it was time to work on this, I lay on my back, with Dale at my head and Ellen right beside me. The others were close by, touching me, and I could feel their love and energy. Immediately, I felt a wrenching heartbreak around all that had happened with my daughter.

I began to sink into the pain and started sobbing. Then I felt a tear from Dale's eyes fall on my face. In that moment, I felt his pain merge with mine. Beyond that, I sensed an empty place inside Dale, and felt myself drawn into that emptiness. Then the space opened wider and wider. That empty place in Dale became a doorway through which I was drawn. Beyond my pain and Dale's pain, into a space of All Pain—the pain of the world. Then, somehow, all of that pain moved into the vastness of All Compassion.

In feeling my pain around my daughter, I became aware of how much I had still blamed myself for all that had happened to her. But in that place of All Compassion, I sensed that perhaps now I could truly forgive myself. Within that deep space, I also relived the cold and terror of my birth. Through this reliving, I perceived how my birth had programmed me with a sense of despair and isolation. I saw, too, how my birth had imprinted feelings of unworthiness, because I felt I must not be worth very much if the reception that I got was that harsh and terrifying.

As I experienced and moved through all of these feelings, I went deeper and deeper into the center of my being. There I had the sense that I had glimpsed my Divine origins—the vastness of my true nature. I had a faint memory of a place of great beauty, love, and light—and, somehow, I was a part of it all. As my awareness came back to the room where I was lying, I felt the love and caring of the people around me. I also sensed that within the depths that I had reached, my pain had been touched and was beginning to heal.

By 11:00 pm, I couldn't wait to crawl into my sleeping bag. I was in the kitchen when Dale came over and started throwing out one probing question after another. I could have clopped him one. I did feel the deep caring behind the questions—his wanting to help me get free. But at that time of night? Naturally my patterns and defenses were squirming from all of that poking and prodding, and they weren't about to go down without a fight.

Those questions churned inside me all night and I woke up feeling yucky. Tears flowed often that day, continuing to wash away the pain that for so long had been buried deep within me. At one point, I shared some insights regarding the hurt and fear that had become undammed. I referred to some things that had happened to me, and suddenly I realized that this was exactly how I viewed these events—as if I'd been a passive recipient. Then, almost as if I were hearing someone else's voice, I heard myself say, "I'm not a victim."

I began to realize that what was breaking free was not only a deep well of fear and pain, particularly involving feelings of not being OK, but also a rock-hard core of resistance. Much of that resistance involved clinging to self-images (especially a "victim-rising-to-hero" syndrome), which had become so habitual that I was barely aware of their presence. Because these images had become so much a part of me, stepping back from them enough even to acknowledge their existence filled me with panic. Deep inside, I felt trapped, entangled in all of this—but I didn't know how to get free.

It was Ellen's openness at the previous Heartwork Intensive about facing things in her life that had given me the courage to begin admitting to myself that this stuff was there. It was difficult even to look. I didn't like what I saw. It felt so unauthentic. And I certainly didn't want anyone else to see it. Beneath all of this was my great longing to be free of everything that wasn't real—and those two forces had been waging a battle inside me.

On the drive home, I thought about how whenever I feel pain, I find myself moving into that deep space where my pain merges with All Pain and then All Compassion, as it did when Dale and I were working. I felt the pain flowing out from my center into the Universe, and I realized that I don't have to hold onto it anymore. I began to sense myself as a flow of energy that has a body to move around in. At my solar plexus is the apex of a cone that opens wider and wider, connecting me to the vastness. Energy from the Universe flows into the cone, then out again, as if there's an infinite cone of energy emerging from my center.

The next day, I felt totally drained, as if I was being flushed out. Defenses and patterns that I hadn't even consciously worked on were crumbling. It felt good to let it all go, not resisting. And I realized that if I did try to resist, it wouldn't do any good. I was too exhausted to hang onto anything.

I woke up later in the week feeling strange and shaky. I found it impossible to stay focused at work. I couldn't shake the mounting sense of anxiety, and I felt as if I was disintegrating, dissolving into nothingness. A flash came of a conversation that I'd had with my son in which he'd said, "The fear is that if I let go of all the guilt and pain, there won't be anything left. And it's terrifying!" I felt like a clam that had lost its shell. I didn't know who or what I was. I desperately grasped for something that was true, something that I knew for sure that I was. I found myself saying, "I am Divine love and light, I am Divine love and light...." Now it's one thing to affirm that on an ordinary Thursday afternoon. It could be rather reassuring. But when I couldn't find one single thing to say about myself except, "I am Divine love and light," it catapulted me right into the center of pure terror.

The next day, I called Dale and told him what I'd been experiencing, and he replied, "There's strength in the terror—in that place of Not Knowing. That is your true self. That is home. The questioning, 'Who Am I?' is the path Home. Surrendering totally into the not knowing is the heart of our work on ourselves." It was exactly what I needed to hear. I wasn't going crazy. Terrifying as it all felt, what was happening was part of what needed to happen. This was a stage in my journey.

Later that day, I left for a weekend retreat at the Omega Institute. If I hadn't already paid for it, I doubt that I would have gone. I didn't feel like being with anyone. I wasn't sure that I knew how to be with anyone—or even how to be. Although Omega had come to feel like home to me, I arrived there feeling like a stranger in a strange land.

It was as if I were seeing everything for the first time. With each new being that I met—tree, flower, person, spider—I felt a pause within me. Then from that pause would emerge a sense of awe and wonder, followed by a feeling of, "Who am I with this?"

I was seeking nothing. (It felt as if I'd already had more than I'd bargained for.) And yet each moment held a gift. Sometimes I'd become swept away with the beauty and wonder of it all. Two of my closest friends from home were there, as well as old Omega friends. One friend who'd been on an inner journey of her own looked at me impishly and pointing to my nametag, she asked, "Who's that?" We both cracked up. I said, "I don't know..." And it felt OK not to know. Being was more than enough.

The next day after lunch, I started thinking about the myriad events, thoughts and feelings from birth onward that I've identified with as part of my life. Then suddenly the question surfaced, "Who am I without any of my history?" What a gut-grabber! I started shaking, and felt that familiar churning in my belly—like spaghetti being thrown into a blender. Once again, I was plunged into that awesome terror. But having survived it once, I didn't panic this time. I was able to be with it, sink into it, even welcome it—knowing that what didn't survive the journey into that vast unknown wasn't worth keeping.

Later that afternoon, I went for a swim and found myself swimming way out into the middle of the lake. During the past two summers, I'd gradually made friends with big lakes. But throughout my life, I've been terrified of being out alone in a vast body of water. I've come close to drowning from sheer panic. Yet there I was, swimming out into the lake with joyful abandon—oblivious to how far from shore I was getting. I kept reaching and reaching to embrace the water. I couldn't get enough of that lake. I opened totally to it, immersed myself in its vastness, and then—with one long exhalation—I let go into it in peaceful surrender. I stretched out on my back, and allowed the water to support me, to cradle me. I felt layer after layer of tension dissolve into those healing waters.

I went to a concert that night called "Songs for the Earth, Sea, and Sky," and the music blended with the song to the planet that was rising within me. Afterward, I was drawn to the trees silhouetted against the sky—and to the stars beyond the trees. The night sky seemed to beckon me. I walked out alone into the darkness and was overcome with the splendor, the awesomeness, of the night. Yet, at the same time, the night felt safe and nurturing. I breathed in the darkness, embraced it, allowed it to envelop me, until I became one with the night. I went to sleep out under the stars.

Sunday morning, I awoke at dawn and climbed the hill to the new meditation cabin. When I opened the door, a flower, a crystal and plain white walls met my eye. I sighed, thinking, "Ah, emptiness." In meditation, I felt a deep sense of peace, and was aware of a different quality to my breathing. Each exhalation was expanding, purifying. Each inhalation was a gift.

I walked out into the sunlight. All around me, the morning was dancing to the music of the angels. My heart leaped to the rhythm, and I became part of the dance. I kept *walking, enveloped in ecstasy. I sensed myself as energy and sensed the energy of the trees and flowers. Everything was dancing to the symphony of the spheres. Facing any terror was worth even just one moment of this.*

Then, at some point, I had an awareness that what I was experiencing was arising from something beyond facing terror. Something had transpired in my surrendering to the vastness of the lake and the night. A part of me had been shattered—the resistant part, the part that felt separate. It was as if I had died to the darkness. Then, from deep inside me, these words arose: "I embraced the night and found the morning."

In the next few weeks, I realized that what occurred at the Heartwork Intensive was a catalyst for some incredibly powerful transformative force that swept through me—a force so powerful that I couldn't even imagine resisting it. I no longer felt that I had to hold myself, or anything else, together. I could just let go and be. And I didn't care what I had to let go of, or what I had to go through to release it. I just never, ever, wanted to go back to the way it was. I knew then what Dale meant when he said, "There's no great loss without a great gain."

About six months later, I began facing and accepting aspects of my shadow self that I had previously denied or hadn't seen clearly. As I became more comfortable with my shadow side, I allowed myself to do such "unspiritual" things as releasing buried rage and spitting out my most horrible fantasies—and loving myself at the same time. Then the "bad" stuff would go "poof" and I would think, "Did I once believe that I was so awful because of that?" I then found myself relaxing into a quiet, loving space with myself where I experienced a greater sense of integration and wholeness. It was very healing to love all of me. And as I increasingly opened to myself with honesty and compassion, I found my heart opening to others in the same way.

It's now been about ten months since my first Heartwork Intensive. For the past two weeks, I've been quietly breathing my way into the depths of my vulnerability. My breath pushes deeper into the resistance that prevents me from opening totally to the whole of the human condition. I feel the boundaries of my heart dissolving as it ceases trying to keep out the pain—and simultaneously ceases to wither. As my heart opens to the pain, I feel it blossoming.

My breath bores deeper into the tightness in my gut, until the bottom drops out of my belly. Because my heart no longer tries to shut out the pain, my belly no longer tries to contain it. My resistance falls into the abyss. There is nothing except my exposure. I feel as if I'm lying naked, spread eagle.

All the while, my body is quivering and tears rise as from some underground spring. Though I've never felt so exposed, I'm here with it so totally that seeking to make it otherwise is not part of this moment. This moment is for feeling the precariousness, the poignancy, of being a human being at this time on our planet. I feel it all—and I'm still here, in this body. With all that we've survived together, this body and me, did I really think that we wouldn't make it through this?

With no pushing and no feeling of urgency, I sense the terror beginning to move out into the vastness. I wait—and out of my vulnerability, I feel my strength arising.

Love after Love

The time will come
when, with elation,
you will greet yourself arriving
at your own door, in your own mirror,
and each will smile at the other's welcome,

and say, sit here. Eat.
You will love again the stranger who was your self.
Give wine. Give bread. Give back your heart
to itself, to the stranger who has loved you

all your life, whom you ignored
for another, who knows you by heart.
Take down the love letters from the bookshelf,

the photographs, the desperate notes,
peel your own image from the mirror.
Sit. Feast on your life.

—DEREK WALCOTT

PART IV: THE EVOLUTION OF HEARTWORK

Into each of us,
God has poured
a mystery—

our nose follows
its scent:

Raisin bread in
the toaster,
Spring daffodils yellow
in the afternoon rain.

From sun up
to sun down
we follow this trail
of scattered gold and rubies.

Don't waste this
precious time indoors
with idle toys
and mindless distraction!

Before you know it
the bell will ring;
the game is up,

and none of us
wants to be left
standing alone,

not knowing which way
is Home.

—RICHARD WEHRMAN

THE EVOLUTION OF HEARTWORK

Heartwork's story began as my story. I was born on July 3, 1945. This is the 61st year of my existence as Dale Loren Goldstein.

My current life began on July 3, 1969—my 24th birthday—when I woke up to the fact that I had not really been alive since I was nine years old (the age when I became so terrified of death that a cloud descended over my life). I had recently graduated from social work school and was on the first leg of a cross-country trip with my wife. It was my first summer vacation in ten years, and I was excited about having the freedom to experience the beauty and adventures the trip promised. We stopped first in Chicago to visit good friends we hadn't seen in a year. Our friends were deeply involved in the politics of the '60s, and we spent many long hours talking politics and listening to rock and roll music—mostly the Moody Blues' *In Search of the Lost Chord* and *On the Threshold of a Dream*.

We had intended to stay only one day, but we ended up staying three. On that last day (my birthday), with little sleep, lots of emotionally charged conversations, and the time just being "right," I had what the father of humanistic psychology, Abraham Maslow, called a peak experience. My realization was not all that profound from the outside—I simply saw that I had been treating my wife (and all women) chauvinistically. I realized I had been creating a separation based on gender that for me prevented women from existing as real beings. This consequently prevented me from having real relationships with them. What was infinitely more important and exciting than the realization itself was the internal state that opened for me. For the first time since I was nine, I felt fully alive. I was ecstatic. This, I realized, was what I had been searching for, even though I hadn't known before that I was searching for it.

The "high" lasted a few days and then dissipated. But I was forever changed. I knew that I wanted to live my life fully alive, and I began searching for a way to recapture and hold onto that experience.

WHEN THE STUDENT IS READY, THE TEACHER APPEARS

The dissatisfaction of my "half-life" created problems in my marriage, and my wife and I decided to seek counseling. I called a trusted psychotherapist and psychology professor who was the only person I had met at that time who had spoken what I perceived to be Truth. His wife answered the phone and told me that he was in Japan, sitting in a Zen temple for a year. She recommended that we call Fred Thompson, a close friend and colleague.

Fred became my first real therapist and my first spiritual teacher. He taught me how to meditate, and he gave me a more spacious perspective on life that took me beyond the rational, linear, conceptual world I had believed to be reality up to that point.

About a year and a half after my peak experience, I had what I refer to as my "religious experience." I was riding in a car with a friend of my housemate's when "the sky opened up." The words that came out of my mouth were, "This is it! This is it! Why couldn't I see it before when it was right in front of my eyes?" To this day, I don't really understand what happened or why, but what I can say is that the veils of conditioned perception lifted and for the next two weeks, I was seeing things-as-they-are. I lived in a world where everything made sense, fit together perfectly. In some very real sense, I was a holy (wholey) man. Wherever I went, things came into order—even the traffic lights would turn green as I approached them. It was a magical world. I saw *how* everything connected to everything else—present, past and future. Kids would ask me about God (although I knew nothing about God), and people would come to me with their problems and those problems would be resolved without my saying a word. I did nothing. I just watched in awe as it all unfolded before my eyes: the Great Mystery.

And then I lost it. Gradually, over a week or so, I watched paradise fade beyond my grasp. Losing this state of being was the most excruciatingly painful experience of my 25 years of life. I went into a deep depression. I asked all my friends how they would feel if I killed myself. I wasn't really considering suicide—I was too emotionally dead to do that. I was just trying to find someone who could help me. They all became afraid except for Fred, who looked at me and said, "Well, I'd kind of miss your form." I had no idea what he was talking about, but I knew he wasn't afraid. So I asked Fred if I could stay with him until I got myself back together. He said that I could, so I moved into his apartment.

Fred was a very brilliant and gifted man, and he tried everything he could think of to lift me out of my depression. Nothing worked. After a week of trying, Fred packed up his suitcase and walked out of his apartment saying, "Boy, I've had enough of messed up people." This was the most helpful thing anyone had ever said to me. I realized that no one else could get me out of my malaise—that I had to do it for myself! So I packed up my things and returned to my home and began piecing my life back together—a reintegration that took a good ten years.

SPIRITUAL TRAINING

One day in the winter of 1970, Fred invited me to go with him to a workshop at the University of Michigan with Philip Kapleau, the author of *The Three Pillars of Zen*. I was excited to experience a real Zen teacher. Roshi Kapleau seemed to understand what I had seen and much more, so I decided to move to upstate New York to undertake Zen training with him at the Rochester Zen Center.

I practiced Zen for 10 years. It was an exercise in extreme frustration. All of my friends and relatives except one got the "Zen prize"—the highly coveted *kensho* (enlightenment) experience. But for some reason, I was unable to attain this insight. I did, however, learn about pain, patience and perseverance—invaluable life lessons—in spite of, or perhaps because of, my frustration. What I learned about pain by sitting in a full lotus posture for as many as 18 hours a day for seven straight days, *sesshin*[1] after *sesshin*, year after year, was that when I totally surrendered to the pain, I got inside it and became one with it. And then the pain changed into something I could only call intense sensation. In other words, there was no longer anything in my experience that I could call pain. From this opening, I realized that the suffering in my life that I usually thought of as pain was really just my resistance to intense sensation—whether physical, emotional or mental.

After ten years of beating my head against the wall of *Mu* (the *koan*[2] practice I had been assigned by Roshi Kapleau in my first *sesshin* with him), I decided to speak with Toni Packer, who had been my teacher for a year and a half. In a private interview with her during a *sesshin* I fessed up. "Toni, I have to tell you the truth," I said. "*Mu* doesn't mean anything to me." I had never told this to Roshi Kapleau because I was certain he would tell me he couldn't do anything for me then, and I would have to leave. And I was afraid Toni would say the same thing. Instead, she looked at me with great compassion, having watched me struggle and suffer for the last ten years, and said, "Well, then, why are you doing it?" In that moment, the whole world opened up for me and I began to find my own way.

About a year and a half later, I was in another retreat with Toni, who had by then left the Zen Center to establish her own Springwater Center for Awareness and Inquiry. "Just do what you need to do!" Toni encouraged the retreatants. I had heard this admonishment for eleven and a half years at the Zen Center, where it meant, "Stay up all night; take as much pain as you can; push yourself beyond yourself so that you can come to awakening!" But this time, I heard what Toni meant: "Just do what you need to do—and do it with awareness." I understood for the first time that

---

[1]   A *sesshin* is a four- or seven-day Zen retreat.

[2]   "In Zen, a *koan* is a formulation, in baffling language, pointing to ultimate Truth. *Koans* cannot be solved by recourse to logical reasoning but only by awakening a deeper level of the mind beyond the discursive intellect" (Philip Kapleau).

the goal of spiritual practice was not to break through some barrier with the use of brute will, but simply to be profoundly aware of what I was experiencing—to be with what was really happening in the moment. So I began checking in with myself from moment to moment to see what I needed to do. And I gave myself permission to do it! I stopped pushing myself the way I had at the Zen Center, where I would black out repeatedly while sitting upright on my cushion, and I started letting go into the experience of my being in the moment.

Once when I was lying down just being deeply with myself, I "dropped into myself" and experienced the flow of life energy through my being. I felt a deep peace and realized that this was the place where true healing came from. Needless to say, I was greatly encouraged and finally felt like something was opening for me in my spiritual practice. And so my spiritual practice became one of letting go with awareness into my experience of the moment. Most of what I have learned that is of value to me has come from this simple, although not easy, practice.

A key example of this came after I attended an Inner Quest Intensive at the Kripalu Center in Lenox, Massachusetts. The intensive was very powerful and at the end of the three days, we did a very beautiful lying-down meditation in a darkened room. The assistant facilitators covered us with blankets, put an object on our abdomens, and told us not to look at the object until they gave us permission. When the meditation was over and we were invited to look at the object, I saw the most compassionate eyes I had ever seen—they were my own eyes. The object was a mirror. A few years later, I went to another Inner Quest Intensive that ended with the same meditation, except that this time when I looked into the mirror, I saw my father's eyes, filled with doubt, staring back at me. Blown away, I returned to Rochester and went to see Toni, thinking I would need years to work through this doubt. She looked at me closely and asked quite simply, "Is that doubt there now?" It wasn't. And that was that! It was a potent lesson about letting go of the past and living fully in the present.

DEEP-FEELING WORK

Shortly after I had switched teachers and began working with Toni, a very close friend who had left Rochester to try to heal herself of a potentially life-threatening illness returned after a three-and-a-half year absence. Cathee (not her real name) had healed herself through a deep-feeling psychotherapeutic process and had returned to continue her Zen training. Not having completed her therapy, and having searched Rochester unsuccessfully for a therapist with whom she could work, she asked me if I might be able to provide her with a safe space in which she could facilitate her own process. I agreed to try to do this for her. At the time, I was practicing polarity therapy, a healing art that involves balancing and removing blocks in a person's energy field to allow self-healing. Cathee settled into a comfortable position on my massage table and within five minutes let go into a deep grieving that I had never seen before. Having cried only twice in the previous 20 years, I was deeply touched by what I saw. When she was done crying, I asked her if she might be able to teach me how to do that. She said she could. And so my opening to my deep-feeling process began.

I started working with Cathee in one and then two two-hour sessions each week in her therapy room, a soundproofed, padded-wall "womb" in her basement that was just big enough for two single mattresses, a rheostat-modulated lamp, a wastebasket and a box of Kleenex. I would lie down on my mattress and Cathee would ask me, "What are you feeling?" I would tell her, and she would usually respond with, "That's a thought, not a feeling. What are you feeling?" After a few months of biweekly sessions, I did a personal intensive where I saw Cathee for a minimum of four hours a day at least five days a week for three weeks, with extra sessions if needed. On the last day of the first week, I got in touch with the pain of not being able to feel deeply. The pain was so excruciating that I "dropped" right back into the place where I originally split from myself emotionally—in the crib—and saw my predicament with absolute clarity.

My mother, an essentially loving and good person, was split in her own being. In her heart, she wanted to pick me up and hold me, comfort me and feed me. But in her head were the voices of her relatives, the pediatrician and the child-rearing authorities of the day—all of whom insisted that babies needed to be kept on a schedule. And because she was split in herself, she was unable to be all there for me emotionally or spiritually, which is mostly what I really needed—a connection to the universe through my mother. And to make matters worse, because she was split in herself, she had a hole in her that she needed to fill—with me! I was all alone and terrified because my life depended on her being there. In that moment of deep pain, I returned to the moment of splitting from myself and cried like a baby—literally, like a baby. And I cried like a baby at least three times a week for the next nine months, twice a week in Cathee's therapy room and the other times with my then-wife Ellen in our bedroom. (Ellen and I would take Friday mornings to do this deep feeling process work together, taking turns letting go into the depths of our feelings until we both felt complete. The unbelievably deep and rich level of intimacy this created led me to formulate the Just Listening tool.)

The most amazing thing happened with this process: by grieving the loss of the "perfect" mother I never had (since no mother can be perfect), I became my own mother. The hole inside me got filled with myself (or the Universe—it's hard to know the difference sometimes). And I learned my first important lesson about deep psychological work: it can have profound positive consequences. Since that time, I have known that I am able to *be with myself* whenever I am feeling fear, grief or incompleteness. And as a result, I am not afraid of others' deep feelings. I have become a good mother, both to myself and to others. I can see and directly relate to the needy little baby in everyone. Far too often, I have observed therapists and teachers distract a client or student from fully experiencing and moving through a deep feeling because it is too uncomfortable for the therapist or teacher. This is a huge disservice to those people they are trying to help, because it deprives them of becoming whole in the place where they split from themselves.

Then my work with Cathee hit an unresolvable snag. In a session with her, I expressed my anger at her for subtly pushing me to go as deep as possible in each session. I had pushed myself all my life, and this was the one place I most did not want to be pushed. Cathee denied she was doing that, and in turn got angry with me. I became enraged at her (which, for shutdown me, was a huge breakthrough) and Cathee walked out of the therapy room. I could no longer continue my work with her because my deep trust in her had been devastated, and I was left feeling very hurt and angry. I also felt unresolved, both in my therapy and in my relationship with Cathee.

Ironically, a few months later I found myself in one of Toni Packer's retreats with Cathee. It was very uncomfortable and distracting to have her in the same sacred space when I was feeling anything but spiritual toward her. One night, when I was doing a walking meditation, I suddenly became aware of Cathee walking toward me, doing her own walking meditation. Fear gripped me, but I had enough presence to ask myself, "What am I so afraid of?" The answer came immediately, "I'm afraid Cathee doesn't love me." And then I was struck with the realization that it didn't matter whether she loved me or not. What I really wanted was to feel connected to her, and I could feel connected to her as long as my heart was open to her—even if her heart wasn't open to me. I also realized that opening my heart to her meant feeling the pain *she* felt from her heart not being open to me. This understanding has served me in all my close relationships ever since.

I continued working with Toni for several more years before it became clear to me that all she was doing for me was pointing me in the direction I was already going. Finally, after one day of a seven-day retreat, I left—not knowing what I would do without a teacher, knowing only that I was tired of pushing against, fighting with and running away from myself. (Although Toni never pushed me in the way my training at the Zen Center did, I had continued to push myself.) And so for the next six days and nights, I did nothing but let go deeper and deeper into my experience in the moment. On the last night of my first solitary retreat, I felt like I was dying. The existential pain of having split from my true nature was absolutely unbearable. When I was finally able to let go into the existential angst of my predicament, every cell of my being lit up, electrified with consciousness. This was a most amazing experience, and further confirmation to continue on this path. For the next dozen or so years, I practiced on my own, doing one or two seven- to ten-day solitary retreats each year. In one ten-day retreat, I surrendered so completely that who I experienced my "self" as being was everything that came into my awareness. In other words, I was equally the bird chirping in the tree and the heart beating in my chest. In this state of awareness, I came to directly know what I can only refer to as the "Supreme Intelligence of Being" that in-forms everything. It was a timeless space that some call the "eternal now" or "the Tao." Having this experience has changed my life and my understanding of who and what we are.

THE FIRST HEARTWORK INTENSIVES

During this period, I had been studying, practicing and teaching polarity therapy. In the summer of 1981, I taught a weeklong advanced polarity therapy seminar at the Omega Institute in Rhinebeck, NY. By then, I had already begun to deviate from the form of polarity therapy taught by my teacher, Dr. Pierre Pannetier. I was doing more of what intuitively felt right—which usually involved sitting at the head of the massage table and lightly holding the client's shoulders and just "being with" the client. I gave a demonstration of Pierre's "general session" of polarity therapy, including about ten minutes of my "being with" the client, and at the end of the demonstration, two women who had the gift of clairvoyance approached me. They both told me that when I was sitting with and holding the client's shoulders, all my chakras (the main energy centers in the human energy system) opened up, merged with and balanced all of the client's chakras. They said the colors and patterns were the most beautiful they'd ever seen. This was just the (external) confirmation I needed! It said, "Trust yourself!" And so, I did. By the next summer at Omega, my work had evolved so much that the week of advanced polarity therapy turned into the first of many Heartwork Intensives (multi-day, residential group workshops that allow participants to concentrate on their process more deeply, often resulting in life-changing breakthroughs). I have been doing Heartwork Intensives ever since.

In 1985, I went through a personal growth training called Lifespring, a life-transforming experience through which I learned many important lessons in a very short time. The most important thing that I got from the Lifespring training was my power and my passion—the driving force behind and the conduit through which the love and compassion I came into this life with could flow. I also stopped being a victim by taking full responsibility for my whole life—among other positive changes. The work I did in Lifespring directly influenced Heartwork Intensives. In the Lifespring advanced training, I saw that the trainer's commitment could have an incredibly powerful effect on individual breakthroughs and on group bonding. And what is perhaps most important, I experienced for the first time the depth of connectedness possible between people. Whereas in meditation retreats I would experience this sense of oneness with the universe, I had never before experienced such oneness with a group of people who were relating to one another on a human level. This experience permanently affected Heartwork Intensives, making them even more powerful.

I invited one of the participants in the Omega intensive, Maribeth Price (who wrote "The Descent," the poem in the beginning of Part I of this book), to attend the new format. The experience was so life-transforming for her that she called me after returning home to Houston, complaining that she could no longer relate to her friends. She asked me if I would come down to Texas and do an intensive for her friends. I have been facilitating intensives, retreats and other workshops there ever since!

TURNING POINTS

It's difficult to look back and remember all the events that have shaped me personally and professionally, but the majority of them seem to be related to the most important people in my life. I am eternally grateful for the close friends and loved ones who have provided me with opportunity after opportunity to grow. A few incidents stand out as either formative or transformative.

I have had to deal with a lot of fear in my life. Fear is the separation from one's true nature, and mine began at birth. I was a big baby (10 pounds, 4½ ounces) and my mother was a little woman (5 feet tall, 100 pounds) who had an intense dislike of pain. As I was coming down the birth canal, pushing along with my mother to get born, she decided she wanted to end the pain and asked to be put out with anesthesia. I felt her "disappear," and I became terrified. I realized that I had to do it on my own, that if I didn't push, I would die. This fear and the beliefs that formed out of the experience (first, that if I didn't push, I would die; and second, that I had to do it by myself) have been running my life to one degree or another ever since. Once in a private interview with Toni during a *sesshin*, I let myself be in the fear. Toni did the most amazing thing; she jumped right into the fear with me. However, there was a big difference between her experience and mine. While I was totally identified with and caught in the fear, Toni was in it, but not of it. Witnessing this was hugely liberating for me, for I saw the possibility of a way out of my dilemma. A few *sesshin* later, I had the experience of all my fear completely falling away. Almost instantaneously, I had the thought, "Who am I without my fear?" and all the fear came crashing down on me again. Freedom is a long journey!

Much of the fear in my life has centered on my fear of death. When I was nine years old, I was overcome with this fear—why was I born if only to die? I couldn't get any relief or any help from either of my parents. And I couldn't go to sleep at night for fear that I would never wake up again. I realized that if I could keep breathing, I would still be alive in the morning, so I started controlling my breath—a practice which created a split right in the middle of my being, my diaphragm. This fear of death continued for 30 years. Then, one night Ellen was out with a friend and said she was going to be home by 11:00. I went to sleep early and awakened at 1:00 to find that she hadn't yet returned. I became very scared that something terrible had happened to her—that Ellen had been killed in a car accident or something like that. Having some degree of presence, I asked myself, "What am I really afraid of?" The answer came quickly, "I'm afraid of death." I followed with another inquiry, "What is death? What am I really afraid of?" After awhile, I realized what I was really afraid of was being alone—existentially alone—in the universe, forever. So I inquired deeply into this: "What am I really afraid of? What *is* this aloneness?" After some time with this inquiry, something in my mind opened, and I found myself standing inside a huge sphere (so huge that I couldn't see the top of it) made of overlapping luminescent green plates (and I'm red-green color-blind!). And I was *all alone!* Yet in my aloneness, I was whole and connected to everything in the universe. The next morning, I realized I never had to be lonely again, because I could always be with myself in the aloneness. I have never been lonely since.

My son, Devan, slept in bed with Ellen and me for the first 18 months of his life. One night, I awoke and, looking at him sleeping next to me, realized that I would unhesitatingly give my life for this being. I didn't know I had that degree of selflessness in me until that moment.

Trust has also been a big issue for me. For most of my life, I trusted people too much—blindly even. And I got hurt repeatedly. Finally, after being hurt one too many times, I went to Toni and told her that I couldn't trust people anymore, hoping that she would give me the magic answer to being able to trust again. Instead, she said, "Well, why should you? The ego (the sense of a self that is separate from others) is not to be trusted!" That statement left me even more perplexed than I was before. How could I be close to other people if I couldn't trust them? I struggled with this question for some time before the issue clarified itself. I saw first that what Toni had said was absolutely true, and that what I really could trust was that everyone would hurt me sooner or later (and the closer I got, the sooner they would hurt me). Then I saw that when I told some of these people that they had hurt me, they would say something like, "Oh, Dale, you're too sensitive," or "Grow up!" or "Get a life!" I knew that these people would continue to hurt me, and I simply chose not to be close to them anymore. Others would respond with something that ultimately meant, "I'm really sorry that I hurt you, and I want to look with you at what pain I gave to you because it was too much for me to bear." These people I choose to keep in my life.

I also realized that I had been seeing people with one eye closed—only seeing what was deepest inside them, their loving true nature. I didn't want to see their unresolved pain that they would eventually gift me with. I started seeing people with both eyes wide open, so that I'm not as surprised when they give me this gift. Now, I try to see or sense, in any given moment, whether or not a person is trustworthy. I also saw that I had been closing my one eye to people's unresolved pain because I was still holding out the hope (totally unconsciously, of course) that someone would give me the unconditional love that I always had wanted as a child.

Another insight that came from this issue was seeing that I could only be hurt if I needed something from another person (like unconditional love, for example). If I didn't need anything from the person, but I could see and accept him just as he was, I couldn't be hurt. If he gave me his unresolved pain, I simply had compassion for him in both his pain and his unconsciousness of it, which created his suffering. Additionally, as with the physical pain I experienced in *sesshin*, I saw that it was really my resistance to the pain I was being given that caused the hurt. And the resistance was a result of my clinging to some belief about who I am or the way the world is (or should be), and having that belief challenged.

The other transformational practice I've undertaken is the Diamond Approach, with which I have been involved since 2000. The Diamond Approach was developed by Hameed Ali (who uses the pen name A. H. Almaas), a brilliant and profound man who put together the most exquisite system I have found for accessing the spiritual by working through all the doorways on the psychological level. I have been blessed to work with Alia Johnson, one of his senior teachers and the editor of most of his books, who has been able to see the totality of my being and guide me on this stage of my journey. Of the many insights I have gained from the Diamond Approach, one of the most important is the realization that I needn't try to "get present"—that presence is always here, it's really just a matter of my opening to it. I have developed the ability to open to presence whenever I remember to do so. The Diamond Approach has also helped me understand that soul is embodied presence (fully experiencing presence in one's body—including physical sensations and feelings or emotions). This has allowed me to see and relate directly to everyone's soul, and it has had a huge effect on my work. In fact, all the "I and Thou" relationship workshops, intensives and retreats that I now lead came out of one opening in one meditation in one session of the Diamond Approach.

PARTNERSHIP, REVISITED

When my marriage of twenty years ended, I was heartbroken—absolutely unbearably heartbroken. Ellen had been my best friend for twenty-one years, my life partner and co-creator/co-facilitator of Heartwork. In one fell swoop, I lost all of this and my family, my home and my future. I allowed myself to experience the loss fully. For six months, I cried myself to sleep every night, I woke up crying every morning, and I cried whenever I had a break in the day. People who know me well tell me I grew more in those six months than I had in all the work I had done on myself in the previous 30 years. Anyway, one night I cried all night. In the morning, as the sun rose, a little bird chirped, and there was joy in my heart again.

Soon after, I was faced with the decision of whether I wanted to explore relationships with women or live a more monastic life. I chose the former and asked a few friends if they knew any women who might be a good match for me. One person suggested a woman named Carolyn who I had heard for many years was a superb therapist. I called her, and when I told her who I was and why I was calling, she said, "Dale Goldstein! I've been in love with you for 15 years!" It turns out we had been at the same therapy marathon weekend fifteen years earlier—she as a participant, I as a friend of the leader. In the course of the weekend, I had done some work with a participant that had touched Carolyn very deeply.

I invited Carolyn over for dinner. After we ate, we went into the living room and I put on a piece of music for her—"Dream Circle," by Steve Roach. A few minutes into the piece, Carolyn said, "Did you hear that passage? That's the sound the stars make." Years earlier, I too had heard the sound the stars and the universe make. So I rewound the tape and listened closely to the passage. Sure enough, it was the same sound! I sat down next to Carolyn on the sofa, looked into her eyes and remembered her—not from 15 years earlier, but from forever! And so began (or perhaps continued) my journey with Carolyn.

As a footnote to that story, the music I played that night was on audiotape. After my experience with Carolyn, I decided I wanted to have the music on CD instead of tape. I searched every possible source in town and online, but couldn't find it anywhere. So I emailed Steve Roach directly, telling him the story and asking him if he knew where I could get a CD. He replied that he had the last copy and that he would send it to me! And so I own the last (autographed!) copy of the CD.

BEING HERE NOW

I wrote this biographical piece in response to requests from people who wanted to know a little more about how Heartwork came into being. I hope the recounting will serve you in some way. One truth is that the past continues to inform our present. Another truth is that all the experiences related here are just that—past experiences. None of them are really alive now. And Heartwork is about being alive now—fully alive, open, aware and present to whatever comes, moment after moment. That is what I truly hope you get from this book.

Late Fragment

And did you get what

you wanted from this life, even so?

I did.

And what did you want?

To call myself beloved, to feel myself

beloved on the earth.

—RAYMOND CARVER

PART V: NOW THE REAL JOURNEY BEGINS

EPILOGUE

*We shall not cease from exploration and the end of all our exploring will
be to arrive where we started and know the place for the first time.*

—T. S. ELIOT

I sincerely hope *Heartwork* has been of some use to you on your journey. Of course, the book is only as valuable as you make it. Remember: You create your own reality. So what reality do you want to create going forward? If you found the tools in this book useful, by all means use them! They can help you re-member on a daily basis who you really are on a deeper and deeper level.

For more information about becoming involved with Heartwork, please visit the Heartwork Institute's website at www.awakentheheart.org.

Blessings to you on your journey.

Dale L. Goldstein, LCSW

GOOD BOOKS FOR HEARTWORK

The Art of Happiness, by the Dalai Lama and Howard C. Cutler (Penguin Putnam, 1998)

The Artist's Way, by Julia Cameron (Jeremy P. Tarcher/Putnam, 1992)

Awakening the Heart, edited by John Welwood (Shambhala Publications, 1983)

Being Peace, by Thich Nhat Hanh (Parallax Press, 2005)

The Dark Side of the Light Chasers, by Debbie Ford (Hodder & Stoughton, 2001)

Diamond Heart Series, by A. H. Almaas (Shambhala Publications, 2000)

Diamond Mind Series, by A. H. Almaas (Shambhala Publications, 2000)

Embracing the Beloved, by Stephen and Ondrea Levine (Doubleday, 1995)

Emmanuel's Book, compiled by Pat Rodegast and Judith Stanton (Bantam Books, 1985)

Focusing, by Eugene T. Gendlin (Bantam Books, 1981)

Getting the Love You Want, by Harville Hendrix (Harper Perennial, 1988)

A Gradual Awakening, by Stephen Levine (Anchor Books, 1989)

Healing into Life and Death, by Stephen Levine (Anchor Books, 1987)

The Hero with a Thousand Faces, by Joseph Campbell (Princeton University Press, 2004)

The Illuminated Rumi, translations and commentary by Coleman Barks (Broadway Books, 1997)

Inner Journey Home, by A.H. Almaas (Shambhala Publications, 2004)

Inner Work, by Robert A. Johnson (HarperSanFrancisco, 1989)

Journey of the Heart, by John Welwood (HarperCollins, 1996)

Keeping the Love You Find, by Harville Hendrix (Atria Books, 1993)

A Little Book on the Human Shadow, by Robert Bly (HarperSanFrancisco, 1988)

Living Buddha, Living Christ, by Thich Nhat Hanh (Riverhead Books, 1997)

Meetings at the Edge, by Stephen Levine (Gill & MacMillan, 2002)

Men and the Water of Life, by Michael Meade (HarperSanFrancisco, 1993)

New and Selected Poems, by Mary Oliver (Beacon Press, 2004)

No Boundary, by Ken Wilber (Shambhala Publications, 1981)

No Enemies Within, by Dawna Markova (Conari Press, 1994)

Nonviolent Communication, by Marshall Rosenberg (PuddleDancer Press, 2003)

Of Water and the Spirit, by Malidoma Somé (Putnam, 1994)

Ordinary Magic, edited by John Welwood (Shambhala Publications, 1992)

Owning Your Own Shadow, by Robert A. Johnson (HarperSanFrancisco, 1993)

A Path with Heart, by Jack Kornfield (Bantam Books, 1993)

Personal Mythology, by David Feinstein and Stanley Krippner (Penguin, 1989)

The Power of Now, by Eckhart Tolle (New World Library, 2004)

Practicing the Power of Now, by Eckhart Tolle (New World Library, 2001)

Radical Acceptance, by Tara Brach (foreword by Jack Kornfield) (Bantam Books, 2004)

The Selected Poetry of Rainer Maria Rilke, edited and translated by Stephen Mitchell (Vintage Books, 1989)

Siddhartha, by Hermann Hesse (New Directions Publishing, 1957)

Start Where You Are, by Pema Chödrön (HarperCollins, 2003)

Tao Te Ching, translated by Stephen Mitchell (HarperCollins, 2000)

The Tibetan Book of Living and Dying, by Sogyal Rinpoche (HarperSanFrancisco, 1994)

Toward a Psychology of Awakening, by John Welwood (Shambhala Publications, 2002)

The Ultimate Secret to Getting Absolutely Everything You Want, by Mike Hernacki (Berkley, 1988)

When Things Fall Apart, by Pema Chödrön (Shambhala Publications, 2000)

Who Dies? by Stephen Levine (Anchor Books, 1989)

The Wisdom of No Escape, by Pema Chödrön (Shambhala Publications, 2001)

Women Who Run with the Wolves, by Clarissa Pinkola Estés (Ballantine Books, 2003)

The Work of This Moment, by Toni Packer (Shambhala Publications, 1990)

PARTING WORDS

Coming and going, life and death:

A thousand hamlets, a million houses.

Don't you get the point?

Moon in the water, blossom in the sky.

—GIZAN, ABOUT TO DIE

Love for Sale

I have become
a merchant of Love,
selling piecemeal from
the trunk of my car.

Hundreds pass me by each day,
so afraid of my ragged joy.
But for those who risk
my Wild-eyed strangeness,
I have a bargain
they could never guess:

Their stopping was my payment,
and in return
I fill their hands
with Rubies and with Emeralds;
Sapphires dripping
like blue fire—

They cry "Enough!"
yet still I pour
the Jewels of my Heart—
falling through their fingers,
gathering like
Spring's blossoms,
drifted
around their feet.

—RICHARD WEHRMAN

$\mathcal{F}$ire

Flames twist together in a passionate dance,
slicing through the blackness they seek to chase away.
Sparks fly into the inky night air,
flaring momentarily in showy scarlet bursts
and then fading to nothing.
The heat embraces me,
seeping into my pores,
as the light flickers across my face,
illuminating what dark corners I might seek to hide.

But I can hide nothing from this fire—
Nor any other—
because even when the eager wood is consumed,
and the flames no longer leap,
and the searing embers have cooled
to feathery gray ash,
the fire has not died.
It has not left.
It has not disappeared.
It has instead penetrated my body
and found its way to my heart,
where it dances still.

—KATY KOONTZ

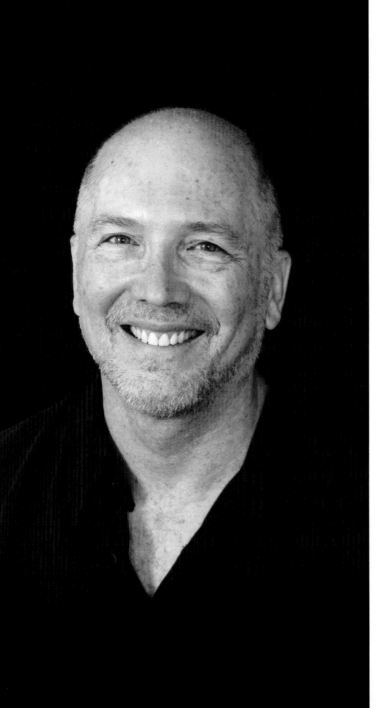

Portrait by Juliet van Otteren

DALE GOLDSTEIN

Dale Goldstein is a Licensed Clinical Social Worker, psychotherapist and workshop facilitator who has actively explored the uses of meditative and psychotherapeutic tools in the process of helping individuals, groups and organizations to heal since 1966.

Dale attended the University of Michigan and Wayne State University, where he received a Master of Social Work degree in 1969. In 1971, feeling a deep lack in his life, Dale moved to Rochester, NY, to practice Zen under the guidance of Roshi Philip Kapleau. In 1980, he changed to a self-inquiry/awareness meditative practice with Toni Packer, with whom he worked for eight more years. Since then, Dale has worked with various spiritual teachers, including Alia Johnson, a senior teacher in the Diamond Approach, with whom he has been working since 2000. He is currently engaged in the Diamond Approach Teacher Training Program.

As a result of his own inner work, which included many years of psychotherapy, Dale saw a need to combine psychological and spiritual work in one comprehensive system. In 1981, he created Heartwork, a gentle yet powerful path for personal/spiritual transformation. Since that time, Dale has been the director of the Heartwork Institute, Inc., home to his private counseling practice and a variety of seminars and workshops that he facilitates internationally.

Dale has written a monthly column entitled "Transformational Journeys" for the *World Times*, the international "good news newspaper," and *New Health Digest*.

> [My life has been] shoshaku jushaku
> (one mistake after another).
>
> —Dogen Zenji

RICHARD WEHRMAN

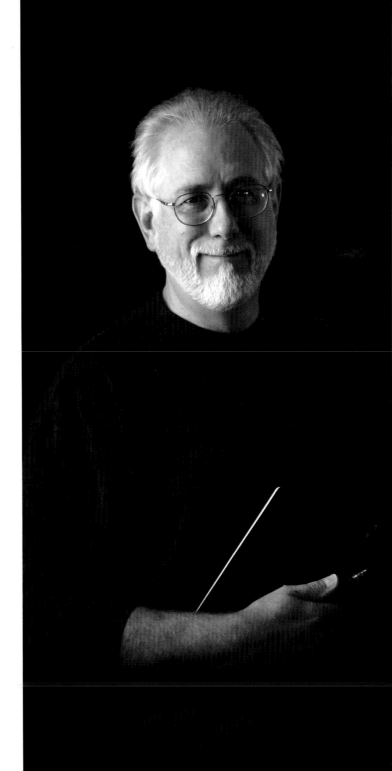

Richard Wehrman was born in St. Louis and attended the Washington University School of Fine Arts, where he studied painting, printmaking and metalsmithing. While living in Missouri, he worked as a silversmith, freelance illustrator and graphic designer. His award-winning paintings have been exhibited at the St. Louis Art Museum, the St. Louis Artist's Guild and Washington University.

In 1973, Richard moved to Rochester, NY, with his wife (illustrator Vicki Wehrman) to study and practice Zen Buddhism with Roshi Philip Kapleau at the Rochester Zen Center. Concurrently, he began a long career as a designer, illustrator and eventually president of the Bob Wright Creative Group. There, he produced award-winning work recognized by the Society of Illustrators, PRINT design annuals, Communication Arts Art Annuals, Graphis Annuals, the New York Art Directors Club and the ADDYs. His illustrations and paintings have been exhibited at the Rochester Institute of Technology, Rochester Nazareth Arts Center, the UNESCO International Poster Show, the Memorial Art Gallery and the Society of Illustrators Gallery in New York. He was chosen as a Rochester Communicator of the Year for illustration and has received a gold medal from the National Society of Illustrators.

Richard is currently absorbed with discovering what it takes, at this late date, to become a real human being. Most of the time, this takes the form of simply getting through the day while causing as little harm as possible to himself and others. In whatever time is left, he creates poetry and graphic art. He serves on the Board of Directors of the Heartwork Institute and lives in (what he hopes will remain) rustic, semi-rural East Bloomfield, NY.

THE HEARTWORK INSTITUTE

The Heartwork Institute, Inc., is a not-for-profit educational organization founded in 1982 to assist people in finding their own paths to wholeness. Heartwork is a way of living that helps individuals find their own natural unfolding or healing process so that they may realize their interconnectedness with all life. The Heartwork Institute, Inc., offers a broad range of programs from individual, relationship and group counseling to personal (one or two people) and group intensives, retreats and workshops which vary from one to ten days in length. The Institute also offers one- to two-year transformational programs. Clients can do counseling in person or via the telephone.

Heartwork is a process of letting go with awareness into the truth of one's being in the moment. In Heartwork retreats, participants gently open through layer after layer of the "false selves" they have created that perpetuate their suffering. In this way, they access the deeper layers of soul and spirit—ultimately coming to directly experience their true nature. Retreats often have themes, such as "Letting Go," "Forgiveness," "Transformation," and "Who Am I, Really?"

In Heartwork Intensives and Weekends of Heartwork, we establish a comfortable balance between individual work, small and large group work and group discussion of content and process. In these breakthrough life-changing events, we use a combination of meditative, psychotherapeutic and experiential tools to move through the internal barriers each of us has unconsciously created that prevent us from having what we *really* want in life. In addition, after all the participants have gotten what they came for (and more), all are given the opportunity to go deep inside themselves and find and claim those aspects of their being that they have not yet owned—the lack of which prevents them from being fully empowered to fulfill their life purpose. Experiencing the deep connection with others that occurs when a group of people come together committed to openness, honesty and getting what they really want forever opens each of the participants to what is possible in relationship.

Everyone essentially wants to love and be loved—but we all build barriers to protect ourselves from being hurt. These barriers not only fail to keep pain out, but they also prevent us from getting the love we really want. Heartwork relationship workshops, which we usually call "I and Thou," thoroughly immerse participants in the use of the Heartwork relationship tools most vital to learning how to move through these barriers and create and sustain growth and intimacy in a relationship.

In Heartwork, we view relationships as primary vehicles for personal and spiritual growth because it is in relationships that most of our personality issues are revealed.

All Heartwork experiences teach participants how to move through self-created barriers in order to open their hearts and minds. From this openness, each of us can find the peace, joy, freedom, aliveness and compassion that is our deepest truth and indeed our birthright. Ultimately, we become enabled to live deeply in this truth, in our life purpose, while in intimate relationships with others.

In addition to the official events offered by the Heartwork Institute, Inc., a great deal of support is offered unofficially and informally by others in the Heartwork community. These people generously share their support, encouragement and guidance based on their own experience with the Heartwork process.

For further information, including greater detail about upcoming programs and events, please contact us at:

The Heartwork Institute
882 Titus Avenue
Rochester, NY 14617
(585) 544-8124
heartwrk@rochester.rr.com
www.awakentheheart.org

Note: We intend to publish numerous versions of *Heartwork*. The editorial content of these versions is exactly the same, but the downloadable internet and coffee table versions in both soft and hard cover feature Richard Wehrman's amazing full-color illustrations. The website will also offer prints, greeting cards, and other items for sale featuring Richard's artwork.

The Heartwork Institute, Inc., is a true not-for-profit organization and operates through sponsorship dues and the generous donations of time and money of people whose lives have been improved by Heartwork. For more information on how you can help out, please visit our website.

CREDITS & PERMISSIONS

The author gratefully acknowledges the following permissions:

ix   Anias Nin, Copyright © by Anias Nin Trust. Reprinted by permission of Blue Sky Press.

2   *The Illuminated Rumi*, translated by Coleman Barks. Copyright © 1997 by Coleman Barks. Reprinted by
       permission of Broadway Books.

4   "The Descent" by Maribeth Price. Copyright © 1982 by Maribeth Price. Used with permission of
       Maribeth Price.

6   "What Does Your Heart Say?" by Richard Wehrman. Copyright © 2002 by Richard Wehrman. Used with
       permission of Richard Wehrman.

9   *The Power of Myth*, by Joseph Campbell. Copyright © 1991 by Joseph Campbell.

11   From both *I Heard God Laughing* and *The Subject Tonight Is Love: 60 Wild & Sweet Poems of Hafiz*,
       translated by Daniel Ladinsky. Copyright © 1996 by Daniel Ladinsky. Published by Penguin Publications and
       used by permission of Daniel Ladinsky.

12   "Singing" by Richard Wehrman. Copyright © 2004 by Richard Wehrman. Used with permission of
       Richard Wehrman.

14   "The Only One Left" by Richard Wehrman. From *What Does Your Heart Say?* by Richard Wehrman.
       Copyright © 2003 by Richard Wehrman. Reprinted by permission of Richard Wehrman.

16   *Letters from The Cosmos*, by Carol J. Swiedler. Copyright © 1993 by Carol J. Swiedler and Edward B. Swiedler.
       Published by Clermont Press and reprinted by permission of Carol J. Swiedler and Edward B. Sweidler;
       (800) 229-1433.

38   "We Are Sailors" by Richard Wehrman. From *What Does Your Heart Say?* by Richard Wehrman.
       Copyright © 2004 by Richard Wehrman. Reprinted by permission of Richard Wehrman.

43   *No Man Is An Island*, by Thomas Merton. Copyright © 1955 by The Abbey of Our Lady of Gethsemani.
       Published by Harcourt, Inc., and reprinted by permission of the publisher and The Abbey of
       Our Lady of Gethsemani.

       Kabir: Ecstatic Poems, translated by Robert Bly. Copyright © 2004 by Robert Bly. Reprinted by permission
       of Robert Bly.

46   "A Simple Death" by Hallie Sawyers. Copyright © 1999 by Hallie Sawyers. Used with permission of
       Hallie Sawyers.

50   "Marriage" by Richard Wehrman. Copyright © 2004 by Richard Wehrman. Used with permission of
       Richard Wehrman.

54   *Emmanuel's Book*, by Pat Rodegast. Copyright © 1985 by Pat Rodegast. Reprinted by permission of
       Random House, Inc.

58   *Letters of Rainer Maria Rilke, Volume Two, 1910-1926*, translated by Jane Bannard Greene and
       M. D. Herter Norton. Copyright © 1948 by Jane Bannard Greene and M. D. Herter Norton. Reprinted by
       permission of W. W. Norton & Company, Inc.

66   "Where Have I Been?" by Philip. Copyright © 2006 by Philip. Used with permission of Philip.

68   "Home" by Richard Wehrman. From *What Does Your Heart Say?* by Richard Wehrman. Copyright © 2004
       by Richard Wehrman. Reprinted by permission of Richard Wehrman.

70   *Letters To A Young Poet*, by Rainer Maria Rilke, translated by Stephen Mitchell. Copyright © 1984. by
       Stephen Mitchell. Reprinted by permission of Random House, Inc.

72   Untitled by Donna Berber. Copyright © 2006 by Donna Berber. Used with permission of Donna Berber.

84   "Winter Morning" by Frances Rapport. Copyright © 2005 by Frances Rapport. Used with permission of Frances Rapport.

87   "Half Light" by Richard Wehrman. Copyright © 2005 by Richard Wehrman. Used with permission of Richard Wehrman.

89   *Rilke's Book of Hours: Love Poems to God*, translated by Anita Barrows and Joanna Macy. Copyright © 1996 by Anita Barrows and Joanna Macy, Reprinted by permission of Penguin Putnam, Inc.

91   Pathwork® Guide Lecture Material. Copyright © 2000 by the Pathwork Foundation. Reprinted by permission of the Pathwork Foundation. (Pathwork® is a registered service mark owned exclusively by the Pathwork Foundation.)

92   *The Enlightened Heart: An Anthology of Sacred Poetry*, by Ghalib, edited by Stephen Mitchell, translated by Jane Hirshfield. Copyright © 1989 by Jane Hirshfield. Published by Harper Collins and reprinted by permission of Jane Hirshfield.

102   "Lovingly Disciplined," by Douglas MacIntyre. Copyright © 2000 by Douglas MacIntyre. Used with permission of Douglas MacIntyre

110   "Saturation Point" by Richard Wehrman. From *The Prisoner's Dream* by Richard Wehrman. Copyright © 2001 by Richard Wehrman. Reprinted by permission of Richard Wehrman.

142   *Collected Poems 1948-1984*, by Derek Walcott. Copyright © 1986 by Derek Walcott. Reprinted by permission of Farrar, Straus and Giroux, LLC.

144   "Mystery" by Richard Wehrman. Copyright © 2004 by Richard Wehrman. Used with permission of Richard Wehrman.

156   "Late Fragment" by Raymond Carver. From *A New Path to the Waterfall,* by Raymond Carver. Copyright © 1989 by Grove/Atlantic. Reprinted by permission of the publisher.

159   "Little Gidding" from *Collected Poems 1909-1962*, by T. S. Eliot. Copyright © 1936 by Harcourt, Inc. and renewed in 1964 by T. S. Eliot. Reprinted by permission of the publisher.

164   "Love for Sale" by Richard Wehrman. From *What Does Your Heart Say?* by Richard Wehrman. Copyright © 2004 by Richard Wehrman. Reprinted by permission of Richard Wehrman.

165   "Fire" by Katy Koontz. Copyright © 2004 by Katy Koontz. Used with permission of Katy Koontz.

PHOTOGRAPHY & ART CREDITS

The illustrator gratefully acknowledges the following permissions:

I: Cover: Wings created from photography copyright © by Mary A. Pen, Tenfour98226@yahoo.com. Used under rights and permissions of www.morguefile.com.

The Blue Marble, image of the Earth from space. NASA Goddard Space Flight Center Image by Reto Stöckli. Complete credits available at: http://visibleearth.nasa.gov/view_rec.php?id=2429.

v: Lily modified from photography copyright © by Elaine Marshall, jmarshall1@sbcglobal.net. Used under rights and permissions of www.morguefile.com.

Lake Michigan, copyright © 2006 by Richard Wehrman (also photography on pages vi, ix, xii and xiv).

3:     Chinese dragon copyright © by Leslie Hender, bohanka@gmail.com. Used under rights and permissions of www.morguefile.com.

Garden, copyright © Photographer: Hans Klamm, Agency: Dreamstime.com.

Footprints, copyright © Photographer: Elena Ray, Agency: Dreamstime.com.

Astrolobe and planters, copyright © 2006 by Richard Wehrman.

4:     Sunrise, copyright © by Manuel Silva, mjas@morguefile.com. Used under rights and permissions of www.morguefile.com.

Water (backgrounds), copyright © 2006 by Richard Wehrman.

Border design modified from artwork copyright © by Aridi Computer Graphics, Inc., www.aridi.com.

6:     Dragonfly wing, copyright © by Anna Kirsten Dickie, anna.dickie@gmail.com. Used under rights and permissions of www.morguefile.com.

Angkor Wat temple doorway, copyright © Photographer: Pavel Bernshtam, Agency: Dreamstime.com.

10:    Crystal, copyright © 2006 by Richard Wehrman.

12:    Water lilies, copyright © 2006 by Richard Wehrman.

19:    Cave image modified from photography copyright © 2003 by Matt Mueller, matt@muellerworld.com.

21:    Sculpted heads modified from photography copyright © by Clara Natoli, clarita1000@gmail.com. Used under rights and permissions of www.morguefile.com.

Clouds, copyright © by John Rivers, doug@ourserendip.com. Used under rights and permissions of www.morguefile.com.

23:    Background fire modified from photography copyright © by Clara Natoli, clarita1000@gmail.com. Used under rights and permissions of www.morguefile.com.

Currency modified from photography copyright © by Nauris, nmy@morguefile.com. Used under rights and permissions of www.morguefile.com.

Automobile modified from photography copyright © by Matt Geyer, matt_geyer@hotmail.com. Used under rights and permissions of www.morguefile.com.

Mansion modified from photography copyright © by Kenn Kiser, kennkiser@yahoo.com. Used under rights and permissions of www.morguefile.com.

Weed, copyright © 2006 by Richard Wehrman.

25:    Bells modified from photography copyright © by Noble Jose, noblejosevu@yahoo.co.in. Used under rights and permissions of www.morguefile.com.

Clock modified from photography copyright © by Dmitry, dzz@mail.ru. Used under rights and permissions of www.morguefile.com.

Barbed wire and chain modified from photography copyright © by Kenn Kiser, kennkiser@yahoo.com. Used under rights and permissions of www.morguefile.com.

Water lily, copyright © 2006 by Richard Wehrman.

27:   Stone wall modified from photography copyright © by Dawn M. Turner, xandert@cableone.net. Used under rights and permissions of www.morguefile.com.

Woman's eye modified from photography copyright © by studio41, studio41@morguefile.com. Used under rights and permissions of www.morguefile.com.

Crystal sphere, copyright © 2006 by Richard Wehrman.

Sky and clouds modified from photography copyright © Dmitry, dzz@mail.ru. Used under rights and permissions of www.morguefile.com.

The Blue Marble, image of the Earth from space. NASA Goddard Space Flight Center Image by Reto Stöckli. Complete credits available at: http://visibleearth.nasa.gov/view_rec.php?id=2429.

29:   Cave wall modified from photography copyright © by Richard van Binsbergen, richard_b@morguefile.com. Used under rights and permissions of www.morguefile.com.

Stones modified from photography copyright © by Carlos, solrac111@gmail.com. Used under rights and permissions of www.morguefile.com.

Shovel, copyright © 2006 by Richard Wehrman.

31:   Candle flame modified from photography copyright © by Julie O'Donoghue, julieorahilly@gmail.com . Used under rights and permissions of www.morguefile.com.

Iron bars modified from photography copyright © by Clara Natoli, clarita1000@gmail.com. Used under rights and permissions of www.morguefile.com.

Lock modified from photography copyright © by jareddeen, jareddeen@morguefile.com. Used under rights and permissions of www.morguefile.com.

Moon images modified from photography copyright © by Razvan Multescu, razvandm2005@yahoo.com and stachoo, stachoo@morguefile.com. Used under rights and permissions of www.morguefile.com.

33:   Golden Buddha modified from photography copyright © by Noble Jose, noblejosevu@yahoo.co.in. Used under rights and permissions of www.morguefile.com.

Spiral Galaxy M101, Hubble Space Telescope Image STScI-PRC2006-10a, NASA and ESA. Complete credits at: http://hubblesite.org/newscenter/newsdesk/archive/releases/2006/10/.

Saint Francis (from the Black Madonna Shrine, Eureka, MO) and glass sphere, copyright © 2006 Richard Wehrman.

Stone arch modified from photography copyright © by Ana, anuska@morguefile.com. Used under rights and permissions of www.morguefile.com.

35:   Sculpted arch modified from photography copyright © by Clara Natoli, clarita1000@gmail.com. Used under rights and permissions of www.morguefile.com.

Sunrise modified from photography copyright © by Patricia, patricia@morguefile.com. Used under rights and permissions of www.morguefile.com.

Bud, water and heart, copyright © 2006 by Richard Wehrman.

36-7 Sunset at Estoril, Lisbon, from photography copyright © by Manuel Silva, mjas@morguefile.com. Used under rights and permissions of www.morguefile.com.

Dharma wheel drawing, copyright © 2006 by Richard Wehrman.

38:   Waves modified from photography copyright © by Manuel Silva, mjas@morguefile.com. Used under rights and permissions of www.morguefile.com.

Water background, copyright © 2006 by Richard Wehrman.

44:   Cave background modified from photography copyright © by Eleanor & Will, wellies@morguefile.com. Used under rights and permissions of www.morguefile.com.

Stones background modified from photography copyright © by Scott Liddell, scott@liddell.com. Used under rights and permissions of www.morguefile.com.

Compass, copyright © Photographer: Steve Simzer, Agency: Dreamstime.com.

Telescope, copyright © Photographer: Peter Högström, Agency: Dreamstime.com.

Other tools, copyright © 2006 by Richard Wehrman.

46:    Girl on beach, copyright © Photographer: Brian Erickson, Agency: Dreamstime.com.

Lily modified from photography copyright © by Elaine Marshall, jmarshall1@sbcglobal.net. Used under rights and permissions of www.morguefile.com.

Border design modified from artwork copyright © by Aridi Computer Graphics, Inc. www.aridi.com.

50:    Rings from photography copyright © by Bianca Meyer geb. Bollmeier, dieraecherin@morguefile.com. Used under rights and permissions of www.morguefile.com.

Wild rose and landscape at dusk, copyright © 2006 by Richard Wehrman.

Border design modified from artwork copyright © by Aridi Computer Graphics, Inc. www.aridi.com.

54:    *Dwarf galaxy NGC 1569*: STScI-PRC2004-06. Credit: ESA, NASA and P. Anders (Göttingen University Galaxy Evolution Group, Germany. Complete credits available at: http://hubblesite.org/newscenter/newsdesk/ archive/releases/2004/06/image/a.

Border design modified from artwork copyright © by Aridi Computer Graphics, Inc. www.aridi.com.

58:    Incense flame, copyright © Photographer: Andres Rodriguez, Agency: Dreamstime.com.

Border design modified from artwork copyright © byAridi Computer Graphics, Inc. www.aridi.com.

66:    Border design modified from artwork copyright © by Aridi Computer Graphics, Inc. www.aridi.com.

68:    Feet in grass and wood floor, copyright © 2006 by Richard Wehrman.

The Blue Marble, image of the Earth from space. NASA Goddard Space Flight Center Image by Reto Stöckli. Complete credits available at: http://visibleearth.nasa.gov/view_rec.php?id=2429.

Border design modified from artwork copyright © by Aridi Computer Graphics, Inc. www.aridi.com.

70:    Border design modified from artwork copyright © by Aridi Computer Graphics, Inc. www.aridi.com.

78:    Feather, copyright © Photographer: Joao estevao Andrade de freitas, Agency: Dreamstime.com.

Frozen waterfall modified from photography copyright © by Kevin Connors, kconnors@kconnors.com, http://www.kconnors.com. Used under rights and permissions of www.morguefile.com.

Ice flow modified from photography copyright © by Porgeir, poxy@morguefile.com. Used under rights and permissions of www.morguefile.com.

Sundial image, modified. Agency: Image provided by Dreamstime.com.

83:    Lake Michigan, copyright © 2006 by Richard Wehrman.

Feather, copyright © Photographer: Joao estevao Andrade de freitas, Agency: Dreamstime.com.

84:    Snow crystals from photography copyright © by Cheryl Rankin, nannabug54@hotmail.com. Used under rights and permissions of www.morguefile.com.

Snow scene, copyright © 2006 by Richard Wehrman.

88:    Buddha carvings modified from photography copyright © by Sanjay Pindiyath, pindiyath@hotmail.com. Used under rights and permissions of www.morguefile.com.

Border design modified from artwork copyright © by Aridi Computer Graphics, Inc. www.aridi.com.

90:    Water lilies, copyright © 2006 by Richard Wehrman.

92:    Image of woman, modified. Agency: Image provided by Dreamstime.com.

Water drops, copyright © Photographer: Mango Loke, Agency: Dreamstime.com.

Rippling water from photography copyright © by Kevin Connors, kconnors@kconnors.com, http://www.kconnors.com. Used under rights and permissions of www.morguefile.com.

102:    Morning glories, copyright © 2006 by Richard Wehrman.

Border design modified from artwork copyright © by Aridi Computer Graphics, Inc. www.aridi.com.

110:    Crystals, sphere and waves, copyright © 2006 by Richard Wehrman.

143:    Boughton Pond, copyright © 2006 by Richard Wehrman.

144:   Crocus, stones and creek, copyright © 2006 by Richard Wehrman.

157:   *Galaxy M101*, Hubble Image: NASA and ESA. For complete description and credits see: http://hubblesite.org/newscenter/newsdesk/archive/releases/2006/10/image/a.

158:   Heart, copyright © 2006 by Richard Wehrman.

160:   Books, copyright © 2006 by Richard Wehrman.
       Border design modified from artwork copyright © by Aridi Computer Graphics, Inc. www.aridi.com.
       Sunset from photography copyright © by David Ellis, Dellis3d@sbcglobal.net.
       Used under rights and permissions of www.morguefile.com.

164:   Boughton Pond, copyright © 2006 Richard Wehrman. Graphic icon modified from artwork copyright © by Aridi Computer Graphics, Inc. www.aridi.com.

165:   Autumn Elms, copyright © 2006 Richard Wehrman. Graphic icon modified from artwork copyright © by Aridi Computer Graphics, Inc. www.aridi.com.

166:   Portrait of Dale Goldstein, copyright © 2006 by Juliet van Otteren. www.jvop.com.

167:   Portrait of Richard Wehrman, copyright © 2006 by Vicki Wehrman.

177:   *Hubble Ultra Deep Field*, Hubble Space Telescope Image. View of nearly 10,000 galaxies found within an area equivalent to one-tenth the diameter of the full moon, NASA, ESA, S. Beckwith (STScI) and the HUDF Team. Complete credits at: http://hubblesite.org/newscenter/archive/releases/cosmology/2004/07/image/a/.

Everything that has a beginning has an end.

—BUDDHA

The end of one thing is the beginning of another.

—ANONYMOUS